Table of Contents

HOW TO LIVE ABOARD A BOAT

The Essential Guide to Living on a Yacht

By Cruising Schatzy

Limit of Liability/Disclaimer of Warranty:

The publisher and the author wish to make clear that this work is provided for informational purposes only. As such, no representations or warranties are made concerning the accuracy or plenum of its contents. In particular, we disclaim all warranties, including, but not limited to, fitness for a specific purpose. No implied or expressed warranty may be created or extended by sales or promotional materials.

The advice and strategies presented within may not universally apply to every situation, and readers should exercise discretion in their application. This written work is sold with the understanding that neither the publisher nor the author is engaged in providing medical, legal, or any other professional advice or services. Should professional assistance be required, it is strongly recommended to consult the services of a qualified and competent professional.

Neither the publisher nor the author shall be held liable for any damages from using this work or its content. Including references to individuals, organizations, or websites within this work, whether for citation or as potential sources of additional information, does not constitute an endorsement by the publisher or the author of the information provided, or the recommendations made by these entities.

Furthermore, readers should be aware that websites referenced in this work may have undergone changes or removal between the time of writing and publication and when it is being read. It is the reader's responsibility to verify such sources' current status and reliability.

INTRODUCTION

The dream

Imagine waking up to the gentle spray of salty breezes, the rhythmic lapping of water against the hull, and the rays of dawn softly streaming through your porthole.

You are not in a conventional home; you have entered a world where your residence is also your means of exploring. A motor yacht is not simply a vessel—it's a haven, an escape, and a means to endless adventures. Here, the rewards are as limitless as the sea itself.

To many, the allure of living on a yacht may be derived from the romanticism of nautical novels and epic maritime tales, especially with swashbucklers and pirates. And sure, there's definitely a touch of that romance—the allure of casting off lines and setting off to distant horizons. But the rewards run far deeper than the surface of all that; it's the chance to live life on your terms.

There is a built-in excitement of waking up in a new location every morning, your windows framing a changing scenery of quaint ports, peaceful anchorages, and idyllic coves. The world is your backyard, and you are the daring explorer charting your course through the world's beauty and wonder. Each day holds the potential for a new adventure full of discovery, whether you find a secluded beach, a bustling fishing village, or a hidden gem such as a restaurant that only the locals know exists.

Beyond the lure of changing scenery, living aboard a motor yacht creates a unique sense of community—a camaraderie or bond among fellow adventurers who share your passion for boating life. Marinas become meeting grounds, where stories are exchanged over sunset cocktails, and laughter mingles with the lapping of waves against the docks and water birds calling overhead. Lifelong friendships are cultivated on these docks as individuals from diverse backgrounds connect to pursue a shared dream.

Adventures aside, perhaps the most understated reward lies in the daily rhythm of life on board. The movement of the tides mimics the rhythm of existence itself. It's a life pared down to its essentials—simple, intentional, and unique experiences. The confined space a yacht provides encourages a minimalist mindset, prompting you to embrace what truly matters and release the physical baggage that clutters modern existence.

This book will dig deeper into the many rewards and benefits accompanying the choice to live aboard a motor yacht, from the practical considerations of downsizing and adapting to life on the water to the unique connection with nature, self, and others.

First Steps

Becoming a liveaboard on a boat can be a dream come true for those with a sense of adventure and the desire to live an unconventional lifestyle. It offers the opportunity to explore, enjoy the freedom of the open sea, and create unique memories. But it can also provide an alternative place to live and, for some, might even be more affordable than living on land.

Moving from a spacious house in the mountains to a medium-sized motor yacht has had its challenges, but the trade-off is the feeling of freedom, and the sense of adventure living on a boat brings. We didn't start the process of wanting to live on a dock, but that is where we ended up due to the twists and turns that life offers when you least expect it. We are so thankful that we chose our 1990 Jefferson 48' Rivanna to be our home and even more grateful that we have a great marina to live in until we set our course for the grand adventure.

Often, when we share with people that we live on a yacht, the response is that they, too, would like to live on a boat. Let's be honest: the fantasy of motoring off into the sunset has its appeal; it's romantic, and the idea of freedom on the seas is enticing. We have found that life aboard a boat has many pitfalls, but at the same time, the rewards seem to exceed the drawbacks.

When we initially set out on this adventure, we had many misconceptions about the boat-buying process, the amount of money required, the type of boat we were buying, and the reality of our expectations. This book will discuss those misconceptions and give insight into tackling those challenges head-on. Perhaps even make the process easier for you.

So, if you're ready to climb aboard on this exciting journey, let's dive in here and explore some essential first steps to help you buy a boat and become a liveaboard. Consider these items just dipping your toes in the water and something to start thinking about as you delve further into this guide.

Define Your Goals and Lifestyle:

Before jumping into the liveaboard lifestyle, define your goals and desired lifestyle. Consider your preferred cruising destinations, the time you wish to spend on the water, and your expectations for comfort and amenities. Also, who will be joining you? Are you going solo, with your partner, or with a buddy? Or are you a family of five like us?

Understanding your goals will guide you in choosing the right boat and planning for your new life on board. Your goals are likely to change the further you get into this process. Be prepared to pivot and be flexible; being flexible is precisely what we had to do, and we are so grateful that we were in the position to bend and flex. Had we not been open to that, we may not have been able to realize our goal of living on a yacht. After all, we didn't move almost three thousand miles across the county to live in a cramped apartment on land. We went through all that for the adventure, even if our adventure looks a little different than what we originally set as our course.

Research and Educate Yourself:

Gaining knowledge about boating and the liveaboard lifestyle is crucial. Research various yacht types, sizes, and features to determine what suits your needs best. Familiarize yourself with navigation, safety procedures, and required maintenance duties. Utilize resources such as books, online forums, and boating courses to increase your knowledge of yacht ownership and living aboard a vessel. Don't forget to join groups on Facebook that align with your goals. You can learn so much from others who are already living your dream. We joined Facebook groups to get immersed in everything boating, including liveaboard groups. We've met some great people and acquired some good information along the way.

Establish a Realistic Budget:

Creating a realistic budget is also one of the most important aspects of becoming a liveaboard. We will mention this a few times in this book. Consider the yacht's initial purchase price, which can be anywhere from $50,000 to 400,000 on average, ongoing maintenance costs, insurance, mooring fees, fuel, and provisions. It would help if you created a spreadsheet to help you develop a complete budget that includes all the expenses to ensure a smooth transition into the liveaboard lifestyle. When creating this budget, be realistic. The rise in our cost of living crushed our initial budget, and we've had to bend, flex, and revise our expectations, goals, and timelines. Also, in the early days, you aren't likely to know what additional needs your budget will require. Even if you plan everything to the finite, there will always be hidden costs. Be sure to include those unwelcome surprises so you aren't caught unprepared.

Engaging with the Boating Community:

Engaging, not just connecting with the boating community, can be invaluable as you begin your liveaboard journey. Attend boat shows, join boating clubs, and participate in local events to meet experienced boaters and learn from their insights. Networking with like-minded individuals can provide guidance, support, and a sense of community. It is also great to have boat buddies for going out on adventures—power and safety in numbers.

Determine Your Yacht's Specifications:

Once you have a clear idea of your goals and budget, start narrowing down your options by determining the yacht specifications for live aboard. Consider factors such as size, layout, accommodation, and amenities. Assess whether you prefer a sailboat or a motor yacht, as each offers different advantages and considerations for the liveaboard lifestyle. Deciding which style of boat is best for you will heavily depend on your end goal. Are you circumnavigating or living in a marina? Do you plan on taking smaller trips? Grander scale trips benefit from wind power, thus necessitating a sailboat or catamaran. If you plan to live on a dock or a mooring ball in a marina and want more luxury or comfort, a motor yacht might be the better choice. When we started our journey, we were set on buying a catamaran, but when it came to buying, we found that the motor yacht was a better match for our family's needs and rapidly changing circumstances.

Seek Professional Guidance:

Engaging the expertise of professionals is highly recommended, especially if you're new to boating. If possible, consult a reputable yacht broker specializing in liveaboard yachts. A knowledgeable broker can assist you in finding the right boat within your budget, handle paperwork, and guide you through purchasing. We have heard so many sad stories about people having many problems with their boat purchase. Be sure to take your time in selecting a good broker. Ask for references, seek out names in the boating community you've joined, and look at the broker's reputation and how long they have been brokering boats. Do not hire the first smooth talker who answers the phone. You want to find someone to work on your behalf. This is just like hiring a real estate agent: find someone you are comfortable with and confident in their ability to help you throughout the process.

Plan for Yacht Maintenance and Upgrades:

Regular maintenance of your investment is crucial for the longevity and safety of you and your yacht. Develop a maintenance plan that includes routine inspections, engine checks, cleaning, and repairs. It's essential to familiarize yourself with the necessary tasks or enlist the help of professionals for more complex maintenance requirements. Also, we will repeat this throughout this book; be sure to have a budget set aside for these costs. We have spent much time and money on simple maintenance items that we can perform ourselves, and the costs add up. Keeping up on a boat is much the same as having a home.

Insurance and Safety:

Ensuring your safety and protecting your investment should be a top priority. Research and obtain comprehensive insurance coverage for your yacht, including liability, property, and personal effects. Whether liveaboard long-term or staying one night as a transient, most marinas require you to carry a minimum amount to dock there. Also, plan to invest in essential safety equipment, such as life jackets, fire extinguishers, emergency signaling devices, and navigation lights; if your boat doesn't already have these items, plan for purchasing and outfitting.

Adapt to the Liveaboard Lifestyle:

As you prepare to transition into the liveaboard lifestyle, be prepared for adjustments and adaptations. Embrace minimalism and declutter your possessions to optimize space on board. Learn provisioning techniques and adapt your cooking methods to suit the galley's (kitchen) limitations. Adopt a sustainable mindset by conserving water and energy and be prepared for the challenges and rewards of living in a smaller living space. It all boils down to changing your mindset. You cannot expect to live the same life on board as on land. No amount of preparation can truly prepare you for the experience.

There are still days when we look at each other and say, "Do we really live on a boat? How did we get here?"

Be ready for the time of your life.

Remember that this is a lifestyle change and should be approached with an open mind and a willingness to change. Though the entire process can be frustrating and fraught with challenges, it can be rewarding and full of memories to last a lifetime. It is by far the craziest thing we have ever done. Especially considering we have three children in tow, it will also be the most memorable thing we have ever done with our kids.

We've also realized that the adventure may not be cruising from port to port but the day-to-day living aboard a boat tied off on the dock, which is the bigger adventure for now. It is anything but what society deems as normal, and that in itself is, in fact, an adventure.

Dispelling Myths

Living Aboard is Not Just for the Rich

Now that you're interested in this lifestyle and want to learn more, let's discuss a few misconceptions most people automatically have when you say *yacht*. When most people think of living aboard a motor yacht, images of opulence, grandeur, and exclusive lifestyles often come to mind. However, it is essential to dispel the notion that this lifestyle is only reserved for the wealthy, privileged, or elite. Living on a motor yacht is not just about glamour or being ultra-rich; it can be a feasible and fulfilling option for average-income individuals who dream of a life on the water.

Let's explore how living aboard a motor yacht is accessible to a broader range of people and offers an alternative way of life.

Contrary to popular belief, affordable options are available for those interested in living aboard a motor yacht. While luxurious mega-yachts may be out of reach for most, there is a diverse range of smaller, more affordable vessels on the market. These yachts can offer comfortable living spaces, essential amenities, and the opportunity to enjoy the boating lifestyle. By shopping the used yacht market, you can find more budget-friendly options to live your dream on the water. In most cases, it costs much less than buying a house and tends to be much easier and quicker. It took us about a month to complete the purchase. It might take longer if you are acquiring financing. What took us the most time was finding the perfect boat for us.

The process was worth it because living aboard a motor yacht can be more cost-effective than living on land. While initial costs may include purchasing the vessel and equipping it with necessary amenities, the ongoing expenses can be significantly reduced. Compared to traditional homeownership, living aboard a motor yacht eliminates property taxes, mortgage payments, and, in many cases, extensive utility bills. If you have a loan on the boat, consider making a sizable down payment to keep the monthly payments low. Marina fees and maintenance costs can also be more affordable than the expenses associated with maintaining a house or rental. With careful planning and budgeting, average-income individuals can manage the financial aspects of living aboard a motor yacht without compromising their dreams.

Some think it's hard to live on a boat; however, we have found that one of the advantages of living on a motor yacht is the opportunity for a simplified and minimalist lifestyle. Downsizing to a smaller living space encourages you to prioritize what truly matters. Living on a boat necessitates decluttering and embracing a minimalist mindset, which can lead to a more fulfilling and less materialistic life. Furthermore, the limited space encourages a focus on experiences rather than possessions, encouraging a sense of freedom and fewer confines.

We had to make a lot of adjustments to our habits. Though we were not maximalists, it was eye-opening when we had to edit our belongings to make sense on a boat. While we have come a long way, we are still learning what we need on the boat and what needs to be disposed of. There was a lot to get rid of, and organization has become of paramount importance. It's great because we embrace the moments without worrying about what we must live without. We initially had a large storage unit with all our most valuable worldly possessions. Over time, that storage unit had become a burden and a constant reminder of a life we left behind. The furniture and home décor would never be a part of our present or future. Paying for a large storage unit month after month and then becoming years was an unnecessary burden on our budget. We finally downsized to a tiny unit housing only the items we could not get rid of, like photo albums, family china, and other heirlooms. The takeaway is that we should have done that edit before embarking on our journey. We could have saved ourselves a lot of money and hassle had we been more realistic about our expectations and reality. The reality was that we didn't need any of the big stuff that we had retained, especially not on a boat.

So, while many believe that we have limited access to amenities and services, the trade-off is that living aboard a motor yacht provides access to waterfront living that might otherwise be unattainable for average-income individuals. Life becomes weighing out what is more important.

Many marinas offer affordable long-term lease options, providing access to laundry facilities, showers, and Wi-Fi. Additionally, public anchorages and mooring fields provide cost-effective alternatives to marina living. These options allow individuals to enjoy waterfront culture, access to watersports, and experience the sense of community that comes with living on the water—all while staying within a reasonable budget.

Living aboard is about embracing a life of adventure and freedom. The ability to navigate waterways and explore various destinations allows for new experiences and exciting opportunities. With the enormous network of waterways throughout the country, countless hidden gems are waiting to be discovered. Alternatively, you can dock and explore your immediate area or use the boat as your residence while you work to pay for your next adventure.

Living aboard a motor yacht is not an unattainable dream limited to the wealthy. Nearly anyone can try this lifestyle and experience the joys of life on the water. By considering more affordable options, managing expenses, and adapting to a minimalist mindset, anyone can turn their dream of living aboard a yacht into a reality.

We sure don't fit into the stereotype of who lives on a yacht and encourage others to explore the incredible possibilities and opportunities.

The Benefits and Drawbacks of Living Aboard a Boat

Let's start off with the positives first:

It does not get old waking up to the gentle sway of the boat in tune with the melodic lapping of waves. Or enjoying a cup of coffee on deck while feeling the sun's warmth on your face or being surrounded by breathtaking views. Yeah, that is something we can't seem to get enough of. Living aboard a boat offers a lifestyle that combines a sense of freedom and the opportunity to enjoy the beauty surrounding you. Even if it is on the dock.

Giving up a large house with plenty of elbow room and feet firmly planted on the ground was a giant leap for us. Going down in square footage and bobbing on the waves took some time to get used to. But as it turns out, we love it! In fact, one of our favorite things to say is we went from living in the mountains to making waves. Living aboard a boat is not for everyone, but the lifestyle may be a perfect fit for a few.

As we've already pointed out, living aboard a motor yacht offers a unique sense of freedom and mobility. Though we choose to live in a marina, our state has many waterways, rivers, and canals that provide an extensive playground for boaters.

Most will agree that yachts are designed with comfort in mind. We jokingly call ours a floating condo, albeit one that offers beautiful living spaces that, in some, can rival those found in high-end homes. From spacious bedrooms (cabins) and bathrooms (heads) to well-equipped kitchens (galleys) and stylish living rooms (saloons), motor yachts provide all the amenities you need for a comfortable lifestyle. Many also feature panoramic windows that offer stunning views. Or you might want to relax on decks perfect for entertaining guests or simply basking in the sun. The oldest kid has figured out how to hang a hammock on the aft (back) deck and has taken many naps there.

With careful planning and budgeting, the lifestyle can be cost-effective compared to traditional land-based living. The maintenance costs of a yacht are generally lower than those commonly found in maintaining a house. However, if you have significant issues, like with the hull, engines, or generator, that can be extremely costly. It sometimes feels like a contradiction. While living aboard a boat can be a cost-effective living situation, the cost to maintain the boat can sometimes break the bank. If you keep your boat in good condition, you can allocate your saved resources toward future repairs. Proper planning and management make boat living affordable without compromising comfort.

Living on a boat also offers a host of health benefits. The serene environment, fresh breezes, and proximity to nature contribute to stress reduction and overall well-being. Physical activities like swimming, kayaking, or paddleboarding are at your fingertips to stay fit and active. We like to head to the beach as often as possible to surf, boogie board, and make sandcastles. The vitamin D-rich sunshine provides numerous health benefits and promotes a positive mood. In our opinion, life aboard can lead to a healthier and more balanced lifestyle.

Here are some of the negatives of living on a boat:

Limited Space and Storage: Living on a boat obviously means having limited space and storage, which can be challenging, mainly if you are used to a larger living area. This is one of the most asked questions: "Where do you put all your stuff?" You must be creative with your storage solutions and prepared to live with significantly less. As we mentioned, if you have belongings you cannot part with, you must find a storage unit or other place to store the things you cannot bring aboard. Our boat has lots of storage, but we've had to use it creatively.

First and foremost, this is a vessel. It's not a house, condo, or apartment, though we use it that way. The available space allocation has to be shared with storing spare parts, tools, and other mechanisms that help to keep the boat running. In our cabins, we have drawers, cabinets, shelves, closets, and nooks and crannies, but even at that, we have to diligently edit what we keep on board constantly. Also, things go overboard regularly. No matter how careful you are, items and people drop in the water.

TIP: Purchase a cross-body bag or fanny pack to stow things like keys, wallets, and phones for safe boarding and departing the boat or walking the docks. Had we done that at the onset, we wouldn't have lost many things like tablets, key cards, and FOBs in the 'drink.'

Maintenance and Repairs: Boats require regular maintenance, which can be time-consuming and expensive. You will need to learn how to take care of your boat and be prepared to handle unexpected repairs and expenses. The handier you are, the less money you pay experts to do the job. Also, learning to be proactive instead of reactive will enable you to keep ahead of the repairs, which tends to keep costs down. We have learned that when something needs repair, get it handled. Sometimes, repairs can take some time or become more extensive than where you started, which means you may not have use of your boat during that time. We've had pesky repairs that kept us on the dock for some time. Not even any local trips.

Weather and Conditions: Living on a boat means increased exposure to elements like wind, rain, thunder, lightning, and waves. You will need to be prepared for sometimes quickly changing weather conditions and be able to handle rough seas. Living on a boat in a colder climate will offer more challenges than in a warmer year-round climate. In a colder climate, you will have considerations like snow and ice to add to the weather conditions. Just as living in a hurricane and tornado-prone area will also require additional planning and safety measures.

Limited Amenities: Boats typically have limited amenities compared to traditional homes. You may need to adapt to a smaller kitchen (galley), limited water supply, frequent pump outs, and fewer electrical outlets. Our boat is spacious but, indeed, not a palatial estate. However, sometimes, we joke that we have more space than many New York apartments offer and for less money. Still, we must constantly be intentional about what we bring on board, have a plan to keep the water tank full, and we can't run multiple devices simultaneously or risk overloading the breaker. The last part is not dissimilar to our first home, a 1934 bungalow where we couldn't run a blow dryer and the microwave at the same time until we rewired the whole house.

Isolation and Distance: Living on a boat can be isolating, especially in a remote location. You may feel cut off from friends and family and miss out on social events and gatherings. Alternatively, when not on an adventure, it sometimes feels lonely despite being on the dock surrounded by other boaters. Finding a balance between solitude, getting off the boat, and exploring is essential.

Navigating Choices: Sailboats vs. Motor Yachts

As you navigate this experience, a pivotal decision must be made: sail or motor? Each vessel type has its own unique qualities and quirks. The yachting world offers two main options—sailboats and motor yachts—each catering to different needs. In this chapter, we'll dive into the differences between these boats and provide information to help you determine the vessel that aligns with your nautical needs.

The Engine and the Wind: A Tale of Two Boats

Sailboats and motor yachts are the epitome of contrasting philosophies on the water. Sailboats, with their canvas sails billowing in the breeze, evoke a sense of romance and a connection with the elements. They harness the power of the wind, inviting you to engage in an intimate dance with nature. The unhurried pace of sailing allows for complete immersion in the journey.

By contrast, motor yachts embody the spirit of expedition and exploration. With engines thrumming, they, too, offer the ability to travel vast distances efficiently while providing comfort and convenience. The freedom to chart your course without relying mainly on the whims of the wind opens up a world of possibilities for those seeking to cover distance quicker and explore diverse destinations without being so interactive with the vessel and, thus, nature.

Selecting between a sailboat and a motor yacht is a personal decision shaped by your preferences, goals, and lifestyle.

Consider the following as you navigate this choice:

Define your primary objective. Are you drawn to the tranquility of sailing and the art of seamanship, or do you envision embarking on voyages with the speed and stability of a motor yacht?

What is your boating experience? Be realistic about your level of expertise. Sailing demands a learning curve in mastering wind, navigation, and sail handling. Unless you are an experienced and skilled sailor, you will definitely need to obtain lessons. Motor yachts are more straightforward, making them an appealing option for newcomers. However, it is advisable to gain training in either option; buying a motor yacht option will not negate that.

What destinations do you wish to visit? Sailboats excel in long distances, coastal excursions, and island hopping, while motor yachts grant access to remote areas and ports that may be out of reach for sailboats due to their draft requirements and limited engine control. Sailboats typically have a deeper draft than motor yachts, so keep that in mind when planning the type of vessel you want and how it matches your intended destinations. In either option, some island hopping will require anchoring out and tendering to shore, as many shorelines are very shallow and will only allow for outboard motor access.

You should also consider the type of lifestyle and onboard experience you seek. Sailboats often require a more immersive connection with boating because of the smaller deck space, working with the sails, and less cabin space for starters. Motor yachts offer more deck space and modern conveniences for a more comfortable lifestyle. The two are vastly different vibes. Motor yachts can sometimes resemble living in a floating condo where a sailboat will be less spacious unless you can afford one with a wide beam and expanded room count.

There are always going to be two camps on sailboats versus motor yachts. It all comes down to preferences and the best match for the job. There is no wrong answer when deciding unless you deviate from focusing on your needs.

TIP: In the case of being torn between the two, don't listen to other's opinions about either type of boat as a viable means for making a decision. You need to stick with your list of needs. After all, it is all about what you need; this is your adventure and experience, no one else's.

Weigh the potential ongoing care and maintenance each vessel requires. Sailboats entail rigging upkeep and knowledge of sailing systems, while motor yachts involve engine maintenance and systems management. Again, gaining knowledge about both will allow you to make an educated decision between the two types of boats.

Consider each vessel type's initial investment, operating costs, and potential resale value.

Many different types and models are available within each category, like monohull sailboats, catamarans with two hulls, and trimarans with three. As for motor yachts, there are many different body styles, such as trawlers, express, flybridge, and sportfishing. This next section overviews the factors to examine when choosing a boat for liveaboard living. Also, take into consideration that while you may think one style is for you, keeping your options open will allow you to find the right fit for you. As mentioned, we started this journey wanting a catamaran and pivoted to a motor yacht with a flybridge.

When we started this process, we agreed that a catamaran would be the best choice for going on a grand adventure. We quickly realized that catamarans and boats, in general, were in short supply at the time, and what was available on the market were the ones that either needed some help or were going to be far too small for the needs of a family of five. The realization came after we had already sold the house, got rid of over half our belongings, and stored the rest in a facility in our hometown. After driving across the country to buy a catamaran, which we were under contract, it was a huge letdown to discover our dream wouldn't be realized—at least not yet. The deal fell through, and after we refocused, we set our sights on sailboats. This led to a broker showing us a vessel that was far too small for our needs; he said, "Have you ever considered a motor yacht? It seems like that would be a better fit for your family." We looked at each other, and at that moment, the lightbulb went off, and we knew our next internet searches would be considerably different. We had been looking at catamarans and sailboats for a year and were no further ahead. Though looking at motor yachts was not a new concept to us, we had considered it in the early days of boat shopping online; yachts did not end up on our radar until the broker suggested it. We knew he was right; we were exhausted and honestly out of options. So, at that point, we were homeless, living in a long-term vacation rental, and desperate to find a boat to call home. Our new search or mission was on, and it took us all over the state, touring one jalopy after another. When we finally located our boat, we had all but given up hope, but we hadn't entirely given up faith that our dreams would be realized. Our patience was running on empty, so our expectations were low when we drove hours to take a tour. After looking at so many awful options, we knew we had finally found our boat the minute we boarded.

Little did we know that the boat we ended up with would be such a fantastic investment, and we had finally found a wonderful place to call home on the water.

Cruising Sailboats

Monohull Cruisers: Monohull sailboats are the most common choice for liveaboards. They offer a certain amount of comfort, with various sizes available to accommodate different needs. They are ideal for long-distance cruising and can provide ample living space, though unsuitable for many passengers unless it is a larger vessel.

Catamarans: Catamarans are known for their spaciousness and stability. They have two hulls connected by a deck and a fun trampoline on the stern (front) of the boat, providing more living space and reducing heel (tilting) while under sail. Catamarans are excellent for those who want a more spacious and stable living environment. We started out wanting a catamaran, but after more research, it became clear that we were not ready for such an undertaking. Another problem was there wasn't enough inventory in our price range. Also, finding a long-term slip for a catamaran in our desired area would be tricky once we realized there were waiting lists, and besides, we weren't taking off immediately for the grand adventure.

Traditional Gaff-Rigged Sailboats: These boats feature classic designs with wooden masts and gaff rigging. While they require more maintenance, they have a timeless charm and are well-suited for those who prefer traditional craftsmanship and an old-world vibe.

Bluewater Sailboats: These sailboats are designed for long-distance ocean voyages and are known for their sturdiness and reliability. They often feature reinforced hulls, self-sufficiency in water and power, and comfortable interiors for extended living aboard. These boats are also pricey; many are custom long-haul boats requiring elaborate sails and navigation equipment.

Trimarans: Trimarans have three hulls, with the two outer hulls providing stability. They are known for their speed and can offer enough room for living aboard. Trimarans are great for those who want a combination of performance and some comfort. These types are a less common selection for liveaboard, especially if they need to be at the dock. This would be a good option for two people on the move.

Steel and Aluminum Sailboats: Chosen for their durability and capacity to withstand harsh weather conditions. These materials for sailboats are ideal for more adventurous people who plan to explore remote or challenging areas. This type of boat is not for the casual sailor who wants a lot of comfort. Though these boats can be acceptable for living aboard, they are not known for comfort as much as for being workhorses and boast certain stamina.

Motor Yachts and other Vessels

Cruiser Motor Yachts: These are probably the most popular choice for long-term liveaboards. Cruiser motor yachts offer a combination of comfort, space, and amenities. They typically feature multiple cabins (bedrooms), a spacious saloon (living room, pronounced salon), and a well-equipped kitchen (galley), and often include outdoor living areas like flybridges and aft (rear) decks. Cruiser motor yachts are suitable for long-term living and accommodate families, couples, or singles.

Expedition Motor Yachts: The expedition motor yachts are designed for adventurers to handle challenging conditions and long-distance cruising. They tend to have hearty construction, large fuel tanks for extended range, and a focus on self-sufficiency with features like water makers (desalination systems), solar panels, and ample storage space.

Trawlers: Trawler yachts are known for their fuel efficiency, stability, and spacious interiors. They are excellent for those who prefer a slower-paced, long-range cruising lifestyle and experience.

Sportfish Convertibles: Designed for anglers who want to live aboard and fish in style. Depending on the size, they usually feature a well-appointed cockpit for fishing, adequate interiors, and staterooms or cabins. This type is generally best for the outdoorsy people who focus on fishing expeditions and will be at sea most of the time. It can serve as a long-term liveaboard, but it's not likely to provide the level of comfort that other varieties offer.

Express Cruisers: These sleek and fast yachts are designed for day trips and short getaways. While not as spacious as cruiser motor yachts, express cruisers offer comfortable living spaces for couples or small families. They are perfect for those who enjoy quick, coastal adventures. That said, if you are fortunate enough to have a generous budget, the larger model express cruisers offer luxury amenities and ample room for multiple people. This type of boat has a separate cockpit and a nice aft (rear) deck for entertainment and hanging out.

Houseboats: This type of boat is a floating home designed for comfortable living on lakes and rivers. They come in various sizes and configurations, with amenities such as kitchens, bathrooms, sleeping quarters, and open gathering spaces. Houseboats are an excellent choice for those who want a waterfront lifestyle but don't need to set a course on a distant adventure. These types also do not go in the ocean. They are a super choice for people with lots of lake and river systems that you can explore by keeping a day boat parked at your houseboat.

Luxury Yachts: For some, opulence and luxury is the goal. For those people, mega yachts offer the highest comfort and extravagance. These yachts often include hot tubs, spacious lounges, multiple staterooms, and professional crews to cater to your every need and whim. Just bring money. For most, this is an unattainable fantasy, but for a few, these yachts can resemble a floating penthouse with all the high-end offerings that go with having that kind of budget.

Custom-Built Yachts: Some liveaboards opt for custom-built yachts designed to their specifications. This allows for a unique living space tailored to individual tastes and needs. This process is costly, like building a custom house, and will take a couple of years to complete. A great choice, though, if you have the time and money to create the boat of your dreams.

So, once you have decided what type of vessel you want to purchase, a sailboat or motor yacht, the next step is choosing the right boat. This is a list of initial things to consider when narrowing your search for the right boat.

Size: The size of your boat will largely depend on the number of people who will be living aboard, as well as your budget. Larger boats provide more living space and amenities but are more expensive to purchase, operate, and maintain. However, smaller vessels may feel cramped and limit your ability to have guests.

Hull Material: Boats can be made of different materials, including fiberglass, wood, aluminum, and steel. Each material has strengths and weaknesses, so choosing a material suitable for your intended use and budget is essential. Fiberglass is the most common material for boats due to its durability, affordability, and low maintenance.

Stability and Seaworthiness: Living aboard requires a yacht that offers stability and seaworthiness. Consider the hull design, weight distribution, and stability characteristics of the vessel. Look for features such as deep-vee hulls or stabilizer systems that provide a smoother and more comfortable ride, especially in rough waters.

Condition: Evaluate the motor yacht's maintenance history and overall condition. Inspect the vessel thoroughly, looking for wear and tear, corrosion, or structural issues. Consider the age of the boat and the frequency and extent of maintenance or repairs required to ensure it will be a reliable and safe living environment no matter how you intend to use the vessel.

Maintenance and Repair: Boats require regular maintenance and repairs, so choosing a boat that is easy to learn to maintain and repair is essential. Look for boats with simple systems and accessible components to make maintenance and repairs easier. If you have experience with maintenance and repairs, this may come easier to you, but for those who are new, choose a vessel that has been well maintained and the systems aren't overly complicated.

Draft: A boat's draft refers to the boat's depth below the waterline. Vessels with a shallow draft are better for cruising in shallow waters and exploring coastal areas, while ships with a deeper draft are better for offshore sailing and cruising.

Systems and Infrastructure: Look at the onboard systems and infrastructure of the boat. Assess the condition and functionality of the electrical, plumbing, and HVAC systems. Consider the capacity of fuel and water tanks and the availability of alternative power sources, such as generators or solar panels.

Layout and Amenities: The layout and amenities of a boat will largely depend on your personal preferences and needs. Some may have multiple cabins and bathrooms, while others may have a larger salon or galley. Consider your lifestyle and how you plan to use the boat to determine the best layout and amenities.

Storage capacity: Living on a boat means you need efficient use of space, so choosing a ship with adequate storage is essential. Look for boats with built-in storage compartments like closets, lockers, and shelves to maximize your usable space. The more nooks and crannies, the more room for you.

Safety: Safety is of utmost importance when living aboard a boat, so it's crucial to choose a boat with safety features such as a sturdy hull, reliable navigation equipment, and adequate safety gear. More about safety features will be discussed in a later chapter.

Range and Fuel Efficiency: Determine the boat's range and fuel efficiency, especially if you plan to explore distant destinations. Consider the fuel capacity and consumption rates to estimate the cruising range between refueling stops. Fuel efficiency is not only environmentally responsible but also helps manage ongoing costs. If you are leaning towards a sailboat, consider the range using sails and, if needed, motor assistance.

Navigation and Electronics: Look at the boat's navigation and electronic systems. Look for features such as GPS navigation, radar, depth sounder, autopilot, and communication systems. Ensure the vessel is equipped with reliable and up-to-date navigational tools for safe and efficient cruising. If the equipment is not up to standards or is outdated, you will need to consider the cost of upgrading when determining what you are willing to pay for the boat.

Deck and Outdoor Spaces: When looking at the deck and outdoor spaces of the boat, assess the size and layout of the cockpit, flybridge, and swim platform. Look for features that enhance outdoor living, such as comfortable seating areas, dining spaces, and water toys or fishing gear storage. How easy is it to board the boat and use the swim platform?

Livability and Comfort: What is the overall livability and comfort of the yacht? Consider natural lighting, adequate insulation to ensure a pleasant living environment and good ventilation. Look for amenities that enhance comfort, such as air conditioning, heating, water making, and entertainment systems.

Budget and Financing: Determine your budget and consider financing options when shopping for a boat. Consider the initial purchase price, ongoing maintenance costs, insurance premiums, and mooring fees. Consult with financial advisors or marine lending institutions to establish a budget that works well with your financial capabilities.

The Boat-Buying Process

Here's a brief overview of the boat-buying process. This outlines the key points of the process as well as a loose timeline. On the pages following this list is a more detailed checklist you will want to customize for your needs. We also have this list on our website that you can download for free.

Remember that no matter what type of boat you plan to purchase, you will need to find moorage (dockage). We recommend doing this first. It will help you narrow down the type and size of the boat and where you will keep it before you set out on your boat-buying adventure.

Research and Planning Phase

Define Your Requirements:

Decide the boat's primary purpose (sailing, cruising, fishing, etc.).

Determine the size range that suits your needs.

Make a list of essential features, amenities, and layout preferences. Compose a detailed list of

must-haves and nice-to-haves.

Decide the number of passengers the boat should accommodate.

Begin to research where you will live on the boat. Many marinas across the county have long

waiting lists. This may determine your timeframe and budget.

Always Be flexible.

Set a Budget:

Establish a budget that not only includes the purchase price of the boat but also recurring

expenses pad the budget for hidden costs (maintenance, insurance, mooring, fuel, etc.) and

include necessary upgrades.

Research Boat Types and Brands:

Explore different types of boats (sailboats, motor yachts, catamarans, etc.).

Research reputable boat manufacturers and models within your preferred category. Watch the

resale market for available vessels.

Attend Boat Shows and Events:

Visit local boat shows and expos to see a variety of vessels and gather information.

Speak with industry experts and experienced boaters to gain insights. Join social media groups.

The following should occur once you have found the perfect boat for you and an offer has been accepted.

Vessel Inspection and Evaluation:

Survey: Hire a qualified marine surveyor to conduct a thorough inspection, including hull,

structure, systems, and safety features.

Review the surveyor's report to identify any potential issues.

This is a list of what the surveyor will look for. This is only an overview of the items and is not as extensive as the surveyor's list.

Physical Inspection:

Inspect the boat's hull, deck, and superstructure for signs of damage, cracks, or corrosion.

Check for water intrusion, soft spots, or rot in wooden components.

Look at the condition of hatches, windows, and portholes.

Mechanical and Electrical Systems:

Inspect the engine(s), transmission, and generator (if applicable) for signs of wear, leaks, or rust.

Check the electrical systems, wiring, and connections for proper functionality.

Sails and Rigging (for Sailboats):

Inspect sails for tears, stains, and general condition.

Examine rigging, mast, and standing rigging for wear, corrosion, and proper tension.

Interior and Amenities:

Consider the overall condition of the interior, including flooring, upholstery, and cabinetry.

Check appliances, plumbing, and fixtures for leaks or malfunctions.

Test lighting, ventilation, and entertainment systems.

Safety Equipment:

Confirm that the boat is equipped with safety gear, including life jackets, flares, fire extinguishers,

and smoke alarms.

Sea Trial:

Arrange a sea trial to evaluate the boat's performance, maneuverability, and comfort on the water.

Test the steering, throttle, brakes, and other controls.

Documentation and Legalities:

Title and Ownership Documents:

Ensure the seller has clear and valid ownership documents (title, registration, and any liens).

Verify that the boat is not stolen or subject to any legal disputes.

Purchase Agreement:

Draft or review a comprehensive purchase agreement outlining both parties' terms, conditions,

and responsibilities.

Escrow or Broker Services:

Consider using a reputable escrow service or broker to facilitate the transaction securely. An escrow service is highly recommended if you aren't going through a brokerage process. All for-sale-by-owner transactions should be processed through an escrow service. It ensures that you pay the proper fees and taxes, that the boat you are buying has a clear title, and that no liens or other liabilities are attached to the vessel. This service will also expose if the boat has been in a significant accident or damaged by a hurricane, for instance.

Negotiation and Closing:

Price Negotiation:

Based on survey findings and market research, negotiate the final purchase price with the seller. Your broker will do this unless you represent yourself in the purchase.

Provision for Repairs:

If the survey reveals issues, discuss with the seller whether they will address the repairs or adjust

the price accordingly.

Deposit and Payment:

Determine the deposit amount and payment schedule, ensuring a secure payment method. If you

are not using a broker, the escrow service you hire will walk you through this.

Closing and Transfer:

Complete the paperwork to transfer ownership, including title transfer, bill of sale, and

registration.

Additional Imperative Considerations:

Insurance: Purchase comprehensive boat insurance to cover accidents, damages, and liability. If you have a lender, this will be secured before closing. It is also advisable to ensure your insurance early in case you have difficulty locating a provider. In some regions, insurance carriers are tough to come by. Many have pulled out of hurricane regions recently.

Mooring and Storage:

Arrange for a suitable mooring or storage location for your boat. In the early stages of the boat buying process, get on waiting lists if you are in a region with limited liveaboard opportunities. If you don't plan to live on the boat full-time, you may have more options available to you, like seasonal dockage and a separate location for storage when not in use.

Maintenance Plan:

Create a maintenance schedule for routine inspections, cleaning, and necessary repairs. This will be covered in more detail later in the book.

Boating Courses: Consider enrolling in boating courses to enhance your skills and knowledge of vessel operation and safety. If you are a practiced seaman, this should be a breeze; however, for those new to boating, this should be mandatory. Just learning how to dock the boat is a skill. If you don't know how to maneuver your boat into a slip, you could cause severe damage to your boat, marina property, or, even worse, someone else's vessel. Also, knowing how to navigate and handle a large vessel through the ocean or river waterways is essential. With learned skills comes confidence that you will need to ensure a safe voyage. Knowing the laws and rules of the water is also imperative, especially when arriving in unfamiliar waters. Being able to handle yourself under pressure and also being able to rely on your crew is important as well.

Checklist When Buying a Motor Yacht for Living Aboard

Remember, this checklist is intended to provide a broad range of ideas for your yacht living experience. Not all items may be feasible or available on a single yacht, so prioritize your preferences and work closely with a yacht broker or manufacturer to find a boat that meets your specific requirements and budget. This list should be customized to meet your particular needs and should only serve as a place to start. A link to download this list is available at the back of the book. For a glossary of terms, go to the back of the book.

Interior Amenities:

Spacious and comfortable cabins

Main suite with ensuite head (bathroom)

Multiple heads (bathrooms) with showers

Full-sized beds or berths as opposed to crew quarters

Ample storage space for personal belongings

Dedicated workspace or office area

Washer and dryer

Built-in entertainment systems (TV, stereo, speakers)

Satellite TV or streaming capabilities

Quality interior finishes and materials

Storage capabilities

Customizable interior layout options (for new boat purchases)

Galley (Kitchen) Features:

Full-sized refrigerator and freezer

Oven and stovetop with multiple burners

Microwave oven

Dishwasher (usually a bonus item)

Ample counter space and storage

Double sink or decent single

Trash Compactor (usually a bonus item)

Wine cooler or beverage refrigerator (usually a bonus item)

Outdoor Living and Entertainment:

Spacious cockpit or deck area for relaxing and lounging

Outdoor dining area with seating

Wet bar or outdoor kitchen with grill

Refrigerator or ice maker

Sun loungers or sunbeds

Outdoor shower

Sometimes extra gear is included in the sale, such as:

Water toys (paddleboards, kayaks, inflatables)

Waterslide or diving board (if applicable)

Fishing equipment and storage

Navigation and Safety:

Up-to-date navigational instruments (GPS, radar, depth sounder)

Autopilot system

Integrated chart plotter or electronic navigation system

AIS (Automatic Identification System)

Quality helm and navigation consoles

Security and surveillance systems

Backup systems for critical equipment

Safety equipment (life jackets, life rafts, EPIRB)

Fire detection and suppression system

Man-overboard (MOB) system

VHF radio

Flares or flare gun

Dinghy

Comfort and Convenience:

Climate control systems (air conditioning, heating)

Good upholstery and comfortable seating

Large windows for natural light and views

Retractable or convertible roofs or sunshades

Hydraulic swim platform or tender lift system

Stabilization system (gyroscopic or fin stabilizers)

Generous headroom throughout the yacht

Centralized control systems (smart home automation)

Integrated audio and video systems throughout the yacht

Wi-Fi and internet connectivity

Energy and Power:

Energy-efficient systems and appliances

Solar panels or other renewable energy sources

Inverter system for onboard power supply

Generators with sufficient capacity

Large battery banks for extended power storage

Storage and Utility:

Ample storage spaces for equipment and supplies

Utility room or workshop area

Dive equipment storage and rinsing area

Fishing gear storage and tackle center

Water maker for freshwater production is great if you intend to live off dock or cruise often

(usually a bonus item)

Integrated vacuum system for cleaning (usually a bonus item)

Aesthetics and Design:

Customizable interior and exterior design options (for new boat purchases)

Luxurious and high-quality finishes and materials

Modern or classic design aesthetics

Custom furniture and cabinetry options

LED lighting systems with various ambiance settings

Well-designed and user-friendly living spaces

Structural and Exterior:

Hull condition (including signs of damage, corrosion, or blistering)

Deck condition (soft spots, delamination)

Windows, hatches, and portlights (seals, functionality)

Railing and safety equipment (stanchions, lifelines)

Canvas (Bimini top, cockpit enclosure)

Swim platform and ladder

Mechanicals and Systems:

Engines (condition, hours of use, maintenance history)

Fuel system (tanks, filters, lines)

Cooling system (hoses, radiators, pumps)

Exhaust system

Propulsion system (propellers, shafts, thrusters)

Steering system

Electrical system (wiring, batteries, charging system)

Plumbing system (water pumps, hoses, tanks)

Bilge pumps and drainage systems

HVAC systems (air conditioning, heating)

Generator (type, capacity, condition)

Windlass (anchor system)

Trim tabs (if applicable)

Fire suppression system

Navigation light

Water maker for freshwater production

Dinghy or tender (if included)

The Cost of Living on a Boat

In this chapter, we'll explore the liveaboard boat budget and how it stacks up against living on land. First, let's discuss the expenses of purchasing a boat and then go from there. As with buying a home, if you want top-of-the-line, be prepared to pay for it. If you want a bargain, be ready to roll up your sleeves and do some work. Boats big enough to live on by nature will not be a bargain purchase. It is an investment, and the more you put into the boat, if you choose your boat carefully, the more you will get out in experiences, and for some, you may retain the value or increase it if you provide upgrades.

If you are the DIY type and have a decent-sized budget and time, this may be an excellent way to get into a boat of your choice. A boat that needs a refit (interior updates and upgrades) should be priced accordingly. Be careful when looking at boats that have not been upgraded, as there may be more significant issues lurking below the waterline. However, the project could be fun if you find a diamond in the rough at a reasonable price. Our boat was in no way a fixer-upper. However, there were some updates that we decided to do to make the boat a comfortable place for our family. The boat had been well-cared for by the owner before us. However, when he acquired the boat, it was rough and neglected. After pouring lots of time and money into the vessel, he left some of the aesthetics for us to take on. Happily, too, because we've been able to put our personal touch on the décor, and our boat feels like a beautiful coastal oasis and perfectly reflects our family.

Now, let's get started with the budget:

The Initial Investment:

YACHT PURCHASE: The first considerable expense is the cost of the yacht itself. Yachts vary significantly in price, depending on size, age, brand, and features. Newer and larger boats tend to be more expensive, while used and older yachts can offer more affordable options. You can pick up a used yacht from fifty thousand to millions.

FINANCING: Many people finance their yacht purchase through a loan, which can spread the cost over several years. Consider interest rates, down payment, and monthly payments when budgeting.

BOAT SURVEY: You can expect to pay around $25-$35 per foot. So, for example, if you purchase a 48-foot boat, that will cost you $1200-1680, depending on the surveyor.

HAUL OUT: Part of the inspection process is to haul out the boat so the surveyor may inspect the hull. While boat yard rates for haul-out vary, you can expect to pay around $400 for a 48-foot.

TAXES AND REGISTRATION: The state's tax, licensing, and registration fees will vary. Check with your state for the costs of purchasing a boat, licensing, and registration. For illustrative purposes, we will use the example of 7% sales tax on a 100k purchase, which is 7000.00. Add licensing, registration, and US Coast Guard documentation, which, again, requirements will vary by state. For this example, we will say the amount would be around $1400.00.

The seller typically pays the broker fee.

Operating Expenses:

DOCKAGE or MOORING FEES: Depending on where you plan to keep your yacht, you may incur monthly or annual fees for a marina slip or mooring buoy. Docking or moorage costs can vary significantly by location and amenities offered. Even if you do not plan to live on the boat full-time, you will still need to plan to store it somewhere.

And to that extent, if you plan to be underway, there will be dockage or mooring fees at some point while adventuring. Plan for those fees when plotting your course. You may avoid those fees, but remember that depending on where you are traveling, it may not always be feasible or safe to anchor out.

MAINTENANCE AND REPAIRS: Yachts require ongoing maintenance, including regular servicing of engines, hull maintenance, and repairs. Budget for routine upkeep as well as unexpected expenses.

INSURANCE: Yacht insurance is essential to protect your investment. The insurance cost will depend on your yacht's value, location, and cruising plans. Because each region will have different carriers, premiums will vary. In most states, if not all, boat insurance is required whether you have a loan or not. It's the law. Most marinas also require a minimum insurance limit when renting a boat slip. In our marina, we are required to have a million coverage, and the marina is named as an additional insured. Coverage for a 48' boat will start around $250.00 per month and go up from there.

FUEL: Fuel costs can vary widely depending on the size and type of yacht and how often and far you cruise. Consider both short-term and long-term fuel expenses. Also, if you choose to go with a sailboat or catamaran, your fuel consumption will vary drastically from that of a motor yacht. You can roughly estimate your fuel consumption based on the formula of taking your total engine horsepower and dividing it by .10 for gas engines or .06 for diesel engines.

Please remember that the above formula isn't precise and is based on opening up the engines at full throttle. Actual consumption will be reduced at lower cruising speeds. This is only meant as a rough estimate for budgeting and planning.

UTILITIES: If your yacht has amenities like air conditioning, heating, and electrical systems, budget for utilities such as electricity and water if not included in your slip rental. Some marinas include water, garbage, Wi-Fi, cable, and various state and local taxes in the quoted rate. Some may charge extra for utilities, so be sure to ask upfront.

POWER: $150-400 depending on the time of year and your needs for AC or Heating, which can cost a fortune when the temps are soaring or plunging. For this, we'll say an average of $250 per month.

PUMP OUT: Many marinas charge around 5.00 per pump out per week, and with the average month having 4 weeks, that's $20.00 per month.

BOTTOM SCRAPING: The amount is based on the length of your boat and whether you have a lot of growth. Another consideration is if you have bow thrusters cleaned or zincs that need replacing. For a boat of about 48 feet in length and an average cleaning without bow thrusters at roughly 2 hours, you should plan on spending around $160-200/month. The fee will also depend on your region. It could be a lot less if you are in an area that doesn't have significant bottom growth. Bottom scraping may only be necessary quarterly or annually in some cooler or low-growth regions. If you are in an area needing monthly cleaning, pad the amount to plan for additional needs, like changing the zinc or extra scraping.

BOAT CLEANING/DETAILING: As with other boat services, boat cleaning is usually charged per foot. Sometimes, you may be charged more if there is a lot of carbon build-up or the vessel takes longer to clean. The per-foot rate varies, but we've seen anywhere from $10-50 per foot on average. So, a 48-foot boat, at $10 per foot, will cost $480.00 per month. To save money, consider having a deep clean performed quarterly, and you do the routine monthly cleaning in the interim.

Lifestyle Expenses:

PROVISIONS: Budget for groceries, dining out, and entertainment expenses while living aboard. Remember that provisioning for longer voyages may require additional planning and costs.

TRAVEL AND EXCURSIONS: Living on a yacht often involves exploring new destinations. Budget for travel and excursions, including entrance fees to attractions and transportation on land. Even if you aren't always underway, exploring the area where you are stationed is a fun way to keep the adventure alive.

COMMUNICATION: Consider costs associated with staying connected, including internet access, satellite communication, and mobile phone plans. When off-dock, keeping the internet accessible may be tricky. There are now some options for boaters to be connected when out at sea, but it doesn't come cheap.

HEALTHCARE: Ensure you have adequate health insurance coverage, especially if you plan to travel internationally. Budget for medical expenses and prescription medications. Many Travel Insurance carriers will insure US citizens only if they are out of the country for an average of six months out of the year. You can perform an internet search for companies that provide international health insurance. If you intend to live on the dock and work a job, check into coverage offered by your employer. If you are over 65, you must check into options for people traveling and are on Medicare. Ensure your coverage extends to your travel destination regardless of your insurance. If you are planning foreign travel, in some cases, it is cheaper to pay cash for services, which you will need to plan for in your emergency slush fund. (see below)

Unexpected Expenses:

EMERGENCY FUND: Maintaining an emergency fund to cover unexpected repairs, medical emergencies, or other unforeseen circumstances is wise. As with the nature of an emergency, you rarely see it coming. Planning for the unexpected gives you peace of mind, allowing you to handle the situation.

DEPRECIATION: Remember that yachts, like any assets, can depreciate over time. Be prepared for potential depreciation when planning your long-term budget. Consider making larger payments to pay down the principal, thus saving interest over time. This will only reduce how much you pay on the boat for the long haul.

FINANCIAL FLEXIBILITY: Financial flexibility is essential when living aboard a yacht. Be prepared to adjust your budget as circumstances change and consider the potential for seasonal expense variations.

It's important to approach this lifestyle with a well-thought-out budget to ensure you can comfortably sustain this way of life. By carefully considering the various costs associated with yacht living and planning ahead, you can make your dream of living on the water a reality while maintaining financial stability. You may even be able to save money by living a minimal lifestyle.

EXAMPLE BOAT PURCHASE BUDGET

So here's how the boat purchase breaks down:

Purchase price: 100,000

Surveyor: $1200

Haul out: $400

Registration and documentation: $1400

Taxes: $7000

Total: $110,000

(Taxes and fees will vary depending on State and local fees.)

EXAMPLE MONTHLY BOAT BUDGET:

Slip fee: $1550

Power: $250

Pump out: $20

Bottom scraping: $160

Boat insurance: $250

Boat cleaning/detailing: $480

Total: $2710.00

The numbers make it easy to see that monthly liveaboard expenses are manageable after your initial investment. We left out things like groceries, health and car insurance, clothing, investments, savings, or entertainment because those are not specific to owning and docking your boat.

How do the monthly liveaboard expenses stack up against your current living expenses? The sample expenses can significantly increase or decrease depending on many variables we've already mentioned. This is meant as only a starting point.

Finding Your Perfect Place to Live on the Water

Another factor to consider, and this is a big one, is where to anchor down. This section will explore some of the best locations for living on a boat to help you find your perfect home on the water.

Coastal Cities and Towns: Coastal cities and towns offer the benefits of city life with the added bonus of being able to live on the water. Many coastal cities and towns have marinas and yacht clubs offering showers, laundry, and electricity. These locations also provide easy access to shops, restaurants, and cultural attractions.

Tropical Destinations: Living on a boat in tropical destinations can be a dream for many boaters. The Caribbean, the Florida Keys, and Hawaii are popular destinations for live-aboard boaters, offering warm weather, beautiful scenery, and crystal-clear waters.

Inland Waterways: Inland rivers, canals, and lakes can provide boaters a peaceful and serene living environment. These locations offer access to freshwater fishing, swimming, and other water activities and opportunities to explore the surrounding countryside.

Island Communities: Islands can provide an idyllic setting for living on a boat, with clear waters, white sand beaches, and a relaxed way of life. The San Juan Islands in Washington State, the Abacos in the Bahamas, and the Virgin Islands are all popular island destinations for live-aboard boaters.

Historic Waterfronts: Living on a boat in a historic waterfront location can provide a unique and charming living environment. Cities such as Charleston, SC, and Annapolis, MD, have historic waterfronts with beautiful architecture, cultural attractions, and great dining options.

Remote Locations: For those seeking solitude and adventure, remote locations such as Alaska and the Pacific Northwest offer stunning natural scenery and abundant wildlife. These locations can be challenging and require advanced boating skills, but they can also provide a unique and unforgettable living experience.

It's important to consider factors such as weather patterns, amenities, and accessibility. Some locations may be more challenging, requiring more advanced boating skills and experience. Researching local regulations and laws regarding liveaboard boating in each place is also essential.

Ultimately, the best location for living on a boat fits your lifestyle, preferences, and budget. That said, living on a boat in a marina or dockage can be the best choice for those just getting started.

Dock Life at a Marina Versus Anchoring

Living on a boat at a marina versus anchoring offshore are two different experiences, each with advantages and disadvantages. In this section, let's explore the pros and cons of dock life vs. anchoring to help you decide which is right for you.

Living on a Boat at a Marina:

PROS:

Amenities: Living on a boat at a marina provides access to amenities such as electricity, water, showers, and laundry facilities. This makes life on the boat more comfortable and convenient. As we've already said, it's like living in a floating condo at times.

Social Life: Marinas are often bustling with activity, and living at a marina provides opportunities to meet other boaters and participate in social events.

Security: Marinas typically have security measures, such as locked gates and security cameras, which can provide a sense of safety and security. You can also have a safe place to deliver your mail and packages.

Services: Many marinas offer services such as boat maintenance and repair, fueling, and pump-out facilities, making boat ownership more manageable and more convenient.

CONS:

Cost: Living at a marina can be expensive depending on location, with fees for slip rental, electricity, and other amenities adding up quickly.

Crowded: Marinas can be crowded and noisy, especially during peak season. This can make it difficult to find privacy and quiet time.

Restrictions: Some marinas have restrictions on noise, pets, and other activities that can limit your freedom on the boat.

Anchoring Off Shore:

PROS:

Freedom: Anchoring out offshore provides a sense of freedom and independence in choosing where to anchor and when to move.

Cost: Anchoring out offshore is often free or much less expensive than living at a marina, making it an attractive option for those on a budget.

Serenity: Anchoring out offshore can provide peace and quiet, away from the hustle and bustle of marinas.

Nature: Anchoring out offshore provides opportunities to connect with nature and wildlife in a way impossible at a marina.

CONS:

Lack of Amenities: Anchoring out offshore means giving up access to amenities such as electricity, water, laundry, shopping, and showers. This can make life on the boat more challenging and uncomfortable.

Weather: Anchoring out offshore exposes you to elements that can be challenging in bad weather or high winds. Not to mention when severe weather conditions occur like hurricanes, typhoons, or in colder climates, ice and snow.

Limited Social Life: Anchoring out offshore can be isolating, with few opportunities to meet other boaters, participate in social events, or even have a meaningful conversation with someone outside your travel companions.

Security: Anchoring out offshore provides less protection than living at a marina, with the risk of theft or there could even be damage to your boat. Also, modern-day pirates are a real and scary threat, and with the economy tanking for many people, more are seeking desperate measures.

Finding a Suitable Marina:

So, just in case you are convinced that the safety and stability of a marina is where you want to start, you may also wonder how you find a suitable marina.

There is a lot to finding the perfect marina for living aboard and what to Consider.

Choosing a suitable marina for living aboard a boat is a critical decision that can significantly impact your overall experience and enjoyment of the lifestyle. A well-suited marina will provide amenities, a supportive community, and a safe and welcoming environment. This section will explore key factors to consider when searching for a marina to live aboard or visit and what to look for to ensure a great experience.

Location and Accessibility: Consider the marina's location concerning your desired lifestyle and needs. Consider the proximity to essential services such as grocery stores, medical facilities, schools, work (if applicable), and recreational activities. Assess the accessibility of the marina, including the ease of navigation, proximity to major waterways, and availability of transportation options for land-based activities.

Amenities and Facilities:

Assess the amenities and facilities offered by the marina. These may include:

Dockage and Services: Assess the availability of slips suitable for your boat's size and draft, as well as the availability of amenities like shore power, water hookups, and pump-out stations. It might also be important that the marina provides necessary maintenance and repair services or access to qualified professionals.

Security and Safety: Check out the marina's security measures, such as whether there's gated access? Are there surveillance cameras and adequate lighting? Is the parking lot gated as well? Assess the safety protocols, including fire prevention and emergency response systems.

Laundry and Showers: Depending on how well-equipped your boat is, there may be times that you need access to laundry or bathrooms off the boat. Check if the marina provides these amenities or if there are nearby alternatives.

Wi-Fi and Communication: Reliable internet access is essential for many aspects of modern living. Inquire about the availability and quality of Wi-Fi at the marina and cellular reception.

Recreational Facilities: Whether it's just you or maybe you have kids or pets, the type of recreational or exercise facilities, such as swimming pools, fitness centers, playgrounds, community barbecues, or picnic areas, might be important to you.

Community and Atmosphere: Living aboard is not just about the physical location but also about the sense of community and camaraderie. Check out the atmosphere and the social dynamics within the marina. Are there regular events or gatherings that encourage interaction among liveaboards? Engaging with a supportive community can complement your experience, provide opportunities for friendship, and create a sense of belonging.

Regulations and Liveaboard Policies: Review the marina's rules and policies regarding liveaboards. Some marinas have specific guidelines, restrictions, or waiting lists for liveaboard status. Ensure the marina's policies align with your desired lifestyle, including the maximum allowable time for liveaboard status and any additional associated fees.

Cost and Affordability: The marina fees and associated costs should be assessed when evaluating different options. Determine if the marina's pricing structure fits within your budget, including slip fees, liveaboard fees (if applicable), and any additional charges for amenities or services. It's important to balance cost and the marina's amenities and services.

Reviews and Recommendations: Seek reviews and recommendations from other liveaboards or boating communities. Online forums, social media groups, or boating associations can provide valuable insights into the marina's reputation, management, and overall livability.

One of the most important parts of living aboard is finding the right marina for docking. It requires careful consideration of various factors like the marina's location, amenities, community, regulations, cost, and recommendations from other boaters. By thoroughly researching and visiting potential marinas in person, you can make an informed decision and find the ideal marina that aligns with your lifestyle and offers a safe place to anchor or tie up.

For those who do not intend to tie up at a marina but anchor out, include some similar questions when looking at places to anchor. Some marinas have mooring fields that are an affordable way to stay a few nights or, in some cases, a few weeks, and then you are permitted to tender to the docks and park your dinghy to head onto land. Often, they include the use of the amenities in the rate. This is an excellent opportunity to be in a safe place, but it allows for a break from the docks.

Setting Up Your Yacht to Make It a Home

Turning your yacht into a comfortable and inviting home is necessary to provide you and your family a floating haven, but it requires thoughtful planning and creative adaptation. While many principles of interior design and layout apply to land-based homes and yachts, there are unique challenges and considerations when outfitting a boat. In this chapter, we'll explore the process of setting up your yacht home, including essential amenities, interior design and layout, and tips for decorating your yacht to enhance aesthetics and functionality.

Interior Design and Layout

Maximize Space: Unsurprisingly, yachts have limited space, so make the most of it. Choose multifunctional furniture and storage solutions that optimize space usage. You can achieve this by purchasing multiple-use items like storage ottomans for the saloon (living room) and baskets that can be organized while utilizing small spaces, for example.

Open Layout: If possible, go for an open layout, creating a sense of spaciousness. Use minimalistic design principles to avoid clutter and keep the space open and airy. Meaning, don't clutter up the room with unnecessary items.

Nautical or Coastal Living themes: Incorporate nautical themes and color schemes that complement the environment. Blues, whites, and natural wood tones often work well together and can generally be considered a classic way to decorate. Consider future resell if you are doing anything like wallpapering or changing out the window coverings. Be careful not to choose things that are so taste-specific that you don't appeal to potential buyers down the road.

Practicality: Prioritize practicality in your design choices. Use materials and furnishings that are durable, easy to clean, and resistant to saltwater corrosion. If you are lake-living, you still have the elements to consider, especially in a cold climate. We've had to replace many items like area rugs and window coverings because our initial choices didn't consider the type of wear we would have. Especially in small spaces, things just get used more. It has cost way more than it would have had we thought through our choices more.

Furniture: Select compact, lightweight furniture that can be securely fastened. Foldable or modular furniture can be handy in small spaces. Also, think about the weight of the furniture. It should be light and not add volume to your room. We replaced the freestanding sofa that came with the boat. In its place, we got a small, lightweight "L" shaped sofa that fits perfectly in the corner of the salon (living room). It's almost as if it were custom-made for the space, but it cost a fraction of the price.

Storage: Invest in ample storage solutions. Utilize built-in cabinets, under-bed storage, and vertical shelving to keep belongings organized and out of sight. When we replaced the sofa, we got one with legs that raised the couch at least 6" off the floor, allowing us to slide clear storage bins underneath. This works great because now our youngest has another place to store his toys, and we have enough space left for a few other containers to store smaller items.

Galley (Kitchen): Equip your galley with essential appliances, cookware, and utensils. Stow items securely to prevent movement while underway. Do not keep things on the countertop that will easily move around. Ensure the cabinets have adequate catches that keep the doors from flying open when the boat is underway or even when it's simply windy. Sometimes, gently bobbing can turn into tossing when on the open waters, and unsecured things will tumble.

Head (Bathroom): Do yourself a favor and install an electric marine toilet (often called a "head"). It is more convenient than pumping the excrement and makes it less of an unpleasant experience. Also, when boat shopping, look for heads with a separate shower. Some boats don't offer a separate shower, meaning the bathroom is a wet head, and you shower in the middle of the head and then must dry the fixtures, walls, and floor off after usage. It's not a bad setup but having a separate space for showering would be preferable. Ensure that you have proper ventilation to prevent moisture buildup. A ventilation fan is best, but second best is having a porthole to open. You can also purchase a small bathroom-sized dehumidifier to remove the extra moisture.

Berths (Sleeping Areas): Provide comfortable bedding to make each bedroom feel like a cozy escape. Coordinate colors and themes to make it aesthetically pleasing. Also, consider custom mattresses for oddly shaped berths. You can also DIY your custom mattress fit by purchasing high-quality memory foam mattresses. You can use an electric turkey carving knife to cut the foam to your custom dimensions. We also purchased long utility scissors that helped carve the shape to fit the berth. Also, invest in blackout curtains that can help with privacy and sleep quality. In a marina, you can't control the light that might beam through the portholes at night. Alternatively, even while on anchor, the bright moon on a clear night will cause a lot of sleep disruption.

Navigation Station: If you're actively going on adventures, ensure the boat has a dedicated navigation station with space for charting devices like GPS, plotters, and communication equipment. A yacht typically has two navigation stations, one outside and one inside. Sometimes, people will clutter the navigation station inside with books, computers, and other items that will disrupt the purpose of the space. First and foremost, this is a vessel. Our boat's navigation station is set up such that we cannot use it for anything else. This wouldn't have been our first choice, but the large wood steering wheel (tiller) has priority.

Safety Gear: We cannot over-emphasize the importance of equipping your boat with necessary safety gear, including life jackets, fire extinguishers, and emergency signaling devices.

Final Thoughts on Decorating for Yachts

Embrace nautical decor elements like marine artwork, shells, and brass accents to create a maritime ambiance. Use LED lighting to save energy and create an atmosphere. Dimmable fixtures can adjust the mood to suit different occasions. We use the dimmer in the saloon (living room) constantly; otherwise, it sometimes looks like dayglow. Also, use lamps where you can to provide task lighting in addition to adding a touch of warmth to the space.

Mirrors and glossy surfaces can make a space feel larger and reflect natural light. Add a mirror to a dark passageway or to a wall in the main saloon to give light movement and the illusion of more space.

Choose marine-grade, UV-resistant fabrics for upholstery and outdoor uses for cushions and upholstery. These materials are designed to withstand harsh conditions, whether in Southern Florida, where you get beating sun year-round, or the Great Lakes, where you will get cold and snowy winters. In extreme weather conditions, it is always best to have a place to store outdoor furniture cushions and pillows. If you don't have a way to store, get furniture covers.

Select flooring materials that are easy to clean and moisture-resistant, such as teak or marine-grade vinyl. Be careful to select products that are not prone to slippage. It is a boat, and water on the floor makes for a dangerous situation, so choose flooring that isn't hazardous when wet.

Add personal touches with family photos or keepsakes but be mindful of clutter. Minimalism helps maintain a clean and serene environment. Plus, boats tend to get dusty. You don't want to dust the clutter constantly. Keep your selections to a minimum and with a purpose. Don't go so minimal that you don't feel at home.

While living aboard, consider potted plants or herbs that thrive in limited space. They can bring a touch of greenery and freshness and help clean your cabin air. Consider a species of plant that doesn't require much maintenance or isn't finicky. We have an aloe plant that is thriving so far, which is a miracle because indoor plants haven't survived in our care in the past.

Remember that decorating a yacht is different from decorating a home on land. The salty nature of life at sea, including motion, humidity, and limited space, requires careful consideration of materials and design choices. Your yacht should not only reflect your personal style but also prioritize functionality and safety.

Living on a Yacht with Kids

A Successful Family Liveaboard Life

Living on a boat with kids can be a unique and rewarding experience, but it also comes with challenges. This chapter will provide tips and tricks to help you create a successful family life while living on a boat. It will be different for everyone, but these things have kept the harmony in our home.

Involve Your Kids: Before moving onto a boat, involve your kids in decision-making. Discuss the benefits and challenges of living on a boat and ask for their input. This will help them feel included and invested in the new lifestyle. Our middle child wasn't on the same page as the rest of us. It has taken a while for him to warm up to living on the boat. We found a few compromises that have made it more tolerable for him. The key is to go into it with low expectations, have open communication, and, most of all, be willing to accommodate and be available to their needs, wants, and concerns.

Safety First: A constant theme in this book. Safety. Safety is always a top priority when living on a boat, but it's especially important with kids. Ensure your yacht has safety equipment, such as life jackets, fire extinguishers, railings, life preservers, and safety nets. Establish clear rules and guidelines for your kids to ensure their safety. Discuss with them the importance of always being alert on deck, especially when it is underway. Establish rules for being on the dock as well as underway. While many rules should remain the same, some additional rules should be observed when it is underway. One rule in particular is no bow riding. In some states, riding on the bow of a boat is permitted. It is a tragedy waiting to happen, no matter the passenger's age; no one should ever ride on the bow of a boat. All it takes is for the boat's bow to hit a wave or wake from another vessel that can throw a passenger off the boat and into the water. Even if they have a safety jacket on, that won't save that person from being sucked under the boat.

We'll leave that there.

When the boat is firmly anchored or on a dock, use your discretion for whoever walks out to the front of the boat. Our rule for the youngest is that he has to have an adult or older sibling to escort him out there with a vest on. Once you have established rules, discuss them regularly. It's that important. Also, have man-overboard drills. Practice the procedure for rescuing someone and rehearse calling for help. It's not the same as using a phone; handheld radio is the method when out of range. Make sure everyone knows what to do in an emergency; this is the first line of defense and is just wise to do. Have a list of phone numbers and radio channels printed, even laminated, and posted in a handy, accessible spot.

Create a Routine: Establishing a set routine can help your family adjust to life on a boat. This includes regular meals, designated study and play, and consistent bedtimes. This will help your kids feel more settled and secure. We have found that living on a boat can cause a lot of distractions. Staying in the routine is critical to keep up with schoolwork, chores, and personal time.

Make Space for Each Other: Living on a boat can be cramped, so creating personal space for each family member is important. Encourage your kids to have their own designated areas to hang out in. Our aft (back) deck is lovely during the temperate weather months and is the perfect hangout for the older kids. The youngest likes to snuggle on his bed, play on his tablet, plunk on the rug in the saloon (living room), and play with building blocks or his little cars. Also, have spaces where they can keep their personal items. This isn't just a drawer or closet space. Find places in their cabins for books, shells, souvenirs from their travels, and pictures of their friends. This will give them a space to call their own.

Keep a Sense of Normalcy: Even though you're living on a boat, it's crucial to maintain a sense of normalcy. This includes continuing with regular activities, such as schoolwork and extracurricular activities. This will help your kids feel more grounded and connected to their previous lives on land.

Embrace Nature: Living on a boat provides a unique opportunity to connect with nature. Encourage your kids to explore the water and wildlife around them and make it a part of your family routine. This will help your kids better appreciate the environment and their new home. We like to walk around our immediate area and check out the water birds and wildlife. It's an excellent way to exercise, too.

Stay Connected: Living on a boat can be isolating, so it's important to maintain connections with family and friends. Make an effort to stay in touch through video calls or visits. Encourage your kids to maintain friendships through social media or online gaming, which may be an unpopular suggestion, but it helps our kids stay in the loop with their peers.

Make plans together: When plotting and planning your next adventure, whether by boat or hopping into a car, include the kids in the process. We try to plan activities with points of interest for everyone, not just a few family members. It's fun to assign different aspects of the experience to each person and see what they come up with. Since we live on-dock for now, our activities often include going to the beach, checking out a local farm, or finding good cafes and coffee shops to do school and work.

All hands-on deck: There is never a shortage of work. Divide the duties and see a sense of pride in the boat develop in the kids. Maintaining a clean white boat is a lot of work, so many hands make lighter work. While most kids run from chores, ours included, hard work and pride in their work is still a good lesson. Keep to a set chore schedule, including laundry, grocery shopping, meal prep, dusting, vacuuming, and cleaning personal spaces and bathrooms. (heads) Reward them with the chance to earn a special activity or a trip to the local ice cream shop.

Keep it fun!

The minute the kids dread living on the boat is when the dream is over. We try to keep the boat as a fun and exciting experience. Once the kids are no longer enjoying their life aboard, we will have to put the dream away and pursue a new one—together. There are many ways to keep the plan alive, though. Keep the dialogue open and honest. Allow the kids to voice their concerns or opinions, but also ask them to be willing to hear your solutions. Sometimes, it might be as simple as staying on land for a few days, taking more time, and staying with the grandparents or friends. When we visit with our family, we are recharged and eager to return to our floating abode. As mentioned above, also include them in making plans for future adventures. This will give everyone something to look forward to and also allow them to feel like their opinions count.

Yacht Living with Pets

Whether you're a dog lover, a cat person, or have other pets, embracing a pet-friendly yachting lifestyle adds another layer to your adventure. In this chapter, we'll explore the enjoyment and responsibilities of yacht living with pets, including creating a pet-friendly environment, ensuring pet care and safety, and understanding legal considerations.

Creating a Pet-Friendly Yachting Environment

Living on a yacht with pets requires a few well-thought-out adjustments to create a safe and comfortable space for your furry friends.

Pet-Proofing: Just like in a home, pet-proof your yacht. Secure loose items that could be knocked over, cover sharp corners, and stow away objects that might harm pets.

Pet-Friendly Furniture: Consider investing in pet-friendly furniture covers or throws that can withstand the wear and tear of claws and paws.

Non-Skid Surfaces: Take a look at your yacht's deck surfaces. If slippery, purchase nonslip mats or strips that can help prevent accidents for you and your pet. This is to avoid a pet overboard situation.

Comfort Zones: Designate comfortable spaces for your pets, such as cozy beds and resting areas where they can relax and feel secure. Also, ensure they have a safe place to be when you are underway. A pet crate or bed designated for the critter is a good idea.

Proper Ventilation: Ensure good ventilation to maintain a comfortable temperature for your pets. Adequate airflow is essential for their well-being since diesel engines often stink the place up. It's a boat; it's going to happen. Just ensure it is well aired for you and the furry passengers.

Pet Gates and Nets: For some boats, it is a good idea to install pet gates or safety nets to prevent pets from falling overboard or to keep them from accessing areas that could be hazardous.

Pet Care and Safety

Taking care of your pets while living aboard a yacht does require some special planning:

Exercise: To ensure your pets get enough exercise on and off the yacht, take them on regular walks when you can access the shore. Find creative ways to provide playtime on the boat deck or in the saloon (living room) and have a special toy that they get to play with for exercise time. For some dogs, swimming can help keep them happy.

Hydration: Always provide fresh water for your pets and monitor their hydration, especially in warmer climates.

Potty breaks: Train your pets to use a designated spot for going potty, etc., such as a designated piece of astroturf on deck when underway. When on the dock, take them regularly to the pet-friendly areas. Please clean up after them.

Grooming: Maintain regular grooming routines for your pets to keep them clean and comfortable. Brushing can also help control shedding and reduce allergens on board.

Healthcare: Keep up on regular veterinary check-ups and vaccinations for your pets. Discuss seasickness prevention with your animal's veterinarian, especially for cats and dogs prone to motion sickness.

Safety Gear: When going ashore, equip your pets with life jackets, identification tags, and leashes.

Legal Considerations: Living aboard a yacht with pets can also involve legal considerations, depending on your location and the regulations in place:

Customs and Quarantine: Be aware of customs and quarantine regulations for pets when traveling across international borders. Before traveling to foreign countries, ensure your pets meet the entry requirements of your destination.

Vaccination and Health Certificates: Keep current vaccination records and health certificates handy for your pets as local authorities require.

Pet-Friendly Destinations: Research pet-friendly marinas and destinations in advance. Some places are more accommodating to pets than others. These days, many beaches do not allow pets. Be courteous and limit beach visitation with your pet to areas designated for our furry friends.

Pet Regulations: Generally, be aware of pet-designated areas when traveling from port to port. Also, observe and respect leash laws.

Waste Disposal: Dispose of pet waste responsibly and per local regulations.

Earning an Income While Living Aboard a Yacht

Living aboard a yacht is a lifestyle choice and is one that does cost money. It can be an affordable option over the high price of home ownership. But unless you are independently wealthy, retired with good savings, or are a social media star, you will also need to work occasionally to support your lifestyle. Now more than ever, the opportunity for entrepreneurs and employees alike to work from home to sustain their maritime dreams is attainable. Here, we'll explore various ways to earn an income while living aboard a yacht, including work that can be done while docked and passive income streams that can support your adventures on the high seas.

Earning Income While Living Aboard on Dock

Remote Work and Telecommuting: Nowadays, many jobs can be performed remotely. Working as a freelance writer, graphic designer, content manager, or consultant in various fields allows you to earn an income from anywhere. All you need is an internet connection, and you, too, can work on your yacht's aft (back) deck.

Charter Yacht Hosting: If your yacht is well-equipped and maintained, you can offer it for charter when you're not using it. Websites like Airbnb for boats and charter platforms can connect you with potential renters, turning your yacht into a revenue generator. Alternatively, if you live on your boat full-time, you can take people out for weekend afternoon tours. Show them some points of interest and serve them some cheese and crackers for that extra touch. Check local regulations and talk to your insurance agent to ensure you cover the legal bases.

Marine Services: If you possess skills in marine repair, maintenance, sewing things like cushions or curtains, painting, hanging wallpaper, or carpentry, you can offer your services to fellow boaters and dockside businesses. Since yachts require constant upkeep, your skills will be valuable and in demand. To work on docks in marinas, you must have insurance and a business license. Check with the marina offices and local business regulations where you plan to work so you can get set up properly.

Online Businesses: Consider starting an online business that aligns with your interests and expertise. Whether selling nautical-themed products, online courses, or virtual consulting services, an online business can be managed from your yacht's saloon (living room).

Earning Passive Income While on Adventures

Stock Market Investments: Invest in the stock market and develop an income-earning portfolio. With the right investments, you can earn dividends and capital gains passively, even while cruising in remote waters. Use online trading platforms for easy management. Or hire a portfolio advisor.

Real Estate Investments: Owning rental properties or real estate investment trusts (REITs) might provide a steady flow of passive income. A Property management company handles the day-to-day responsibilities, allowing you to focus on your adventures. You can also look at renting your property through Air BnB or VRBO without much hands-on involvement.

Blogging or Vlogging: Document your yacht adventures through blogging or vlogging. Over time, you can monetize your content through ads, sponsorships, affiliate marketing, and merchandise sales. Many cruisers have successfully turned their passion for sailing and boating into a sustainable income source. Alternatively, you may have an area of expertise or experience to blog or vlog about. Maybe it's a passion or hobby that can become a monetized activity.

eBooks and Courses: Share your expertise or experiences by creating eBooks, online courses, or instructional guides related to sailing, navigation, or yacht maintenance. Alternatively, if you aren't a boating expert yet, tap into other areas you have expertise. These digital products can be marketed and sold online, generating income while you're away from the dock.

Drop shipping or E-commerce: Manage an e-commerce store with drop shipping, where you sell products but don't handle inventory. Print on Demand is a popular option as well. The most accessible and straightforward route is setting up a shop through Etsy or a website through Shopify. It's as simple as creating your designs and choosing the products you wish to offer through a Print on Demand supplier (POD). Remember that while it is mostly hands-off, you need reliable internet access to market the products and ensure things are running smoothly. The best part, though, is this model allows you to run a business from anywhere, even while exploring remote locations.

Earning an income while living aboard a yacht is possible and can add an extra layer of fulfillment, knowing that you can cover expenses. The key is to find the right balance between work and play, allowing you to navigate both the open waters and the world of entrepreneurship. As you sail towards financial freedom, your yacht becomes a home and possibly a vessel for your financial success.

In addition to working aboard a boat, if you have kids, you may wonder how to educate them. Well, the answer is relatively simple: if you plan to live on the dock permanently and like your school district, your school-age kids can attend school where you are. For us, we prefer the homeschooling route. There are too many options for homeschooling to cover in this section. Your best bet is to determine whether you are a homeschool or brick-and-mortar education family. Depending on which way you decide to proceed, many resources are available online to help you determine your best homeschooling options. If you plan to send your kids to school, the process is even more straightforward as you follow regular enrollment processes set forth by the school district in which you are located. Remember that when you are ready to set course on an adventure, it might be tricky to work with your district to allow your children's absence if it's not during summer break. Plan your adventures and school options according to your goals.

Essential Boat Maintenance and Cleaning Tips

Maintaining your yacht is not just a practical necessity; it's a crucial aspect of responsible yacht living. Routine maintenance tasks, addressing common issues, and being prepared to resolve unexpected problems are essential to keeping your vessel safe, seaworthy, and comfortable. Additionally, knowing how to find reliable marine services is paramount when more extensive repairs or expertise are required. In this comprehensive chapter, we'll delve into yacht maintenance, guiding you through the steps to ensure your yacht remains in optimal condition; here are some essential maintenance tips for living on a boat as follows.

Routine Maintenance Tasks

Regularly clean your yacht inside and out to prevent dirt, salt, and mildew buildup. Use appropriate cleaning products to protect surfaces and upholstery.

Bilge cleaning: The bilge is the lowest part of the boat's hull, where water will accumulate. Keeping the bilge clean is essential for preventing water penetration and damage while maintaining a healthy living environment. So, when water is left to collect, the water can become stagnant and possibly encourage bacteria growth. Run the bilge pump to remove any excess water and keep the bilge clean with a bilge cleaner. Also, consider painting the bilge compartment to keep a clean and sterile appearance.

Inspect the hull regularly: The hull is the outer layer of the boat that comes into contact with the water. Inspect the hull regularly. Look for signs of wear and damage, such as cracks or blisters. If you find anything, have the repairs done promptly to prevent any further damage.

Engines maintenance: The engines are the pulse of the boat, and regular maintenance is imperative to keep them running smoothly. Follow the manuals for recommendations on engine maintenance, including oil changes, filter replacements, and coolant flushes. Regularly check the engines for any signs of wear or damage and repair any issues promptly.

Electrical systems: The electrical systems are critical for living on a boat, and regular maintenance is essential to avoiding issues. Regularly check the battery, wiring, and other components for damage or wear. Simply testing the electrical systems on a regular schedule will help to ensure they are functioning correctly.

Clean and maintain the plumbing: The plumbing system on a boat is essential for a comfortable living environment. Clean the toilets, sinks, and shower regularly with a marine-safe cleaner. Check the hoses and fittings regularly for leaks or damage and replace any worn-out parts promptly. Check pumps, hoses, and water tanks for signs of wear.

Inspect and service the sails and rigging: If your boat has sails, it's essential to maintain them regularly. Check the sails and rigging for needed repairs and replace any worn-out parts promptly. Keep the sails clean and dry when not in use. Check the riggings and other components to ensure they are in proper condition.

Maintain a clean and organized vessel: Living on a boat requires a clean and organized living space. Whether at sea or living on the dock, if you don't keep the boat clean, vermin such as ants, cockroaches, and other unwelcome guests will arrive. Keeping the interior and exterior of the boat clean of food and crumbs will keep it from inviting pests.

Removing the garbage frequently will help to reduce potential issues; don't allow it to accumulate. Declutter regularly to keep the living space comfortable and functional, and keeping it clean will ensure a sanitary environment.

Anchoring Gear: Check anchor chains, lines, and windlasses for rust and wear. Ensure anchors are securely stowed and accessible for quick deployment.

Dealing with Common Issues

Leaks: Address leaks promptly to prevent interior damage. Identify the source of the leak and reseal or replace faulty seals, hatches, or windows.

Engine Problems: Troubleshoot engine issues, such as overheating or unusual noises, and consult your engine manual or a marine mechanic for guidance.

Electrical Failures: If you encounter electrical failures, inspect fuses, connections, and batteries. Keep spare fuses and essential electrical tools on board. Fuses will definitely go out. We order our fuses off eBay as they are not typically found in stores. Keep more spares on hand than you think you will need. Because eventually, you'll run through them and never want to be without replacements.

Plumbing Failures: Leaky plumbing can lead to water damage and mold. Keep spare plumbing parts and tools for minor repairs. Consult a professional for significant issues. Do not leave the problems to deal with at a later date. Fixing the leaks as they happen will ensure the issue doesn't lead to more damage.

TIP: To avoid the sanitation system backing up-do not flush toilet paper down the toilet. Instead, dispose of the tissue in a waste disposal with a lid. Just remember to take out the trash daily or if underway, invest in some airtight canisters to tide you over until you have the opportunity to use a dock garbage.

Navigation Equipment: Familiarize yourself with navigation equipment and have backup navigation tools, such as charts and handheld GPS devices, in case of electronic failures. You need to know how to use a compass and other non-digital devices in case of outages.

Sails and Rigging Issues: Regularly inspect sails and rigging for wear signs and promptly replace damaged components to avoid compromising safety.

Be Prepared to Resolve Issues

Tools and Spare Parts: Maintain a well-organized toolbox with essential repair tools. Keep a stock of spare parts for critical systems such as batteries, fuses, zincs, screws, tubing, hoses, bilge pumps, and water filters. Also, consider products you will use to maintain the systems, like engine oil, barnacle cleaners, and antifreeze. Once you've had a chance to explore your boat's systems, you will have a better understanding of what is required to maintain your vessel. Keep a list of systems requiring special parts and fluids, and always keep those replacements on hand. When setting out on an adventure, stock more items that are harder to obtain, especially if you plan to travel to foreign ports. Getting parts while visiting other countries will otherwise be costly and time-consuming. Planning for every last thing is impossible, but certain parts replacement can be predictable. Just be as prepared as possible.

Repair and Maintenance Documentation: Keep thorough records of your yacht's maintenance history, including service dates, repairs, and part replacements. This will help you maintain an accurate record of the boat maintenance and help you stay on top of the service schedule.

Emergency Procedures: Develop and rehearse emergency procedures for common onboard issues, such as engine failures, man-overboard situations, and fire. Be sure to discuss with the other passengers what to do in case of various scenarios, like when flying on a commercial flight, and they review evacuation procedures. It is good to know that you have prepared yourself and others.

Safety Drills: Conduct safety drills with your crew to ensure everyone knows their roles in emergencies. It is never a good idea to wait until you are in a critical position to sort out emergency procedures. Try throwing a man-overboard line to someone in the water. Practice hailing for help by knowing what channel and who you are contacting. In case of fire, you should have a protocol so the crew or passengers will understand their role and how to handle the emergency. Also, just like changing the batteries on a scheduled basis, like when we have a time change, get your fire extinguishers on the same schedule.

Insurance: Maintain comprehensive yacht insurance that covers potential damages, accidents, and liability. Most, if not all, reputable marinas require a minimum amount of coverage to dock your boat, even for one night. In many states, it is the law.

Finding reliable marine services can be a challenge. Here are some tips for locating services for maintaining and repairing your vessel.

Local Marinas: Seek recommendations from local marinas for reputable marine service providers, including mechanics, electricians, and riggers.

Online Resources: Use online directories and forums to find reviews and recommendations for marine services in your area.

Networking: Connect with fellow yacht owners and sailors to gather referrals and firsthand experiences with marine service providers.

Certifications and Insurance: Verify that service providers hold relevant certifications and are experienced in working on your type of yacht. Also, be sure that the service provider carries Insurance or guarantees their work. Do not have any work done if you are concerned that the provider does not have adequate training and coverage.

Ask for References: Don't hesitate to ask service providers for references or examples of their past work to assess their reliability and quality. Your vessel is a significant investment, and you should ensure that the provider you select will do the job right. Gaining assurance through others who have received quality work will set your mind at ease. Though nothing is ever guaranteed, it will at least weed out the ones with bad business practices.

Emergency Repairs Contacts: Maintain a list of emergency contacts, including marine towing services and local authorities, for quick access in emergency repair situations.

Yacht maintenance is an ongoing commitment that ensures the longevity and safety of your vessel. You will safeguard your investment by performing routine maintenance tasks, addressing common issues proactively, being prepared for unexpected challenges, and finding reliable marine services when needed.

Best Cleaning Practices for Yacht Maintenance

Maintaining a yacht's pristine white glossy appearance is not just about aesthetics; it's also about preserving the longevity and value of your investment. In this section, we'll explore the best cleaning practices for yacht maintenance, focusing on maintaining and caring for the gel coating.

You might wonder what the gel coating is if you aren't well-versed in all the boating terms yet.

The gel coat on a boat is the outermost layer of protective coating applied to the boat's fiberglass hull or deck during manufacturing. It serves both functional and aesthetic purposes. The gel coat is a smooth, glossy finish that provides a durable barrier against the elements, including water, UV rays, and abrasions. This protective layer enhances the boat's appearance and helps prevent damage and degradation of the underlying fiberglass structure. Gel coats come in various colors and can be maintained and restored to maintain the boat's polished look and ensure sound structural integrity.

Tools and Materials

Before jumping into the cleaning process, gather the necessary tools and materials:

Soft-bristle brushes: Use non-abrasive brushes to avoid scratching the gel coat. It is helpful to purchase brushes that are specifically made for delicate surfaces. When boating or auto-specific, the price tends to go up. That said, if you take care of the brushes and keep them from rotting or sitting out in the elements, you should be able to use them for a long time.

Mild detergent: Use a pH-balanced, biodegradable yacht-specific cleaner, or make a mixture of water and mild dish soap. Do not use harsh chemicals all over the boat. If there are tough stains, use a product with light abrasion to remove the stain from only those spots.

Microfiber cloths and sponges: Gentle on the gel coat and effective at removing dirt and grime. You can also cut up an old t-shirt and make it into rags to save money. We also cut some sad-looking towels into the perfect size for drying the boat. Just ensure that whatever you use isn't rough or can cause any scratching.

Hose and bucket: A hose for rinsing and a decent-sized bucket for mixing and carrying cleaning solutions are essential.

Boat wax and polish: A high-quality boat wax and polish will protect the gel coating and restore its shine. Use sparingly; it costs a lot, and a little goes a long way.

Optional: Speed buffer with soft attachments. Do this only if you have experience using a buffer. If you do not feel confident in your skill set with using a buffer or polisher, then leave that to the professionals. You can do more damage than good if you don't possess the necessary skills.

The Cleaning Process

Pre-Rinse: Working in small sections, begin by rinsing the boat with clean, fresh water to remove loose debris, salt, and other particles. This initial rinse helps prevent scratching during the cleaning process.

Soap and Water: Mix a mild detergent and water in your bucket. Using a soft-bristle brush or a sponge, gently scrub the gel coat in small sections, working from the top down. This ensures you don't miss any spots and minimizes the possibility of streaking.

Rinse Thoroughly: After cleaning each section, rinse it thoroughly with fresh water. Use a hose with a spray nozzle to remove any soap residue. Pay special attention to overlooked areas, like corners, crevices, and seams. In hard-to-reach places, use a soft bristle bottle brush. We have found those kinds of brushes can get into crevices without scratching the coating.

Removing Stubborn Stains: For stubborn stains or scuff marks, use a gel coat cleaner specifically designed to remove these blemishes. Follow the manufacturer's instructions, and always test a small, inconspicuous area first to avoid damaging the finish.

Drying: Dry the boat using a clean, lint-free microfiber cloth to prevent water spots. A chamois is also an excellent option for this step. You can also try using a towel, as we mentioned earlier.

Gel Coat Maintenance:

Protecting and Restoring Shine: Once the boat is clean and dry, you should protect and restore the gel coat's shine. Apply a high-quality boat wax or polish using a clean, soft cloth or applicator pad. Follow the manufacturer's instructions carefully and apply in small sections.

Polishing Techniques: When applying wax or polish, use circular motions to ensure even coverage. Work the product until it shines, and always follow the recommendations for curing and buffing times on the product.

Regular Maintenance: Establish a regular maintenance schedule to keep your yacht's gel coat in optimal condition. Depending on the environmental conditions and usage, you may need to wax and polish your boat every few months.

UV Protection: The sun's UV rays can damage your gel coat. Consider using a UV protectant designed explicitly for gel coat surfaces to prevent fading and oxidation. This is especially vital in the blistering hot climates.

To remain budget-conscious, we try to do as much as possible, but there are times when you must employ the services of professionals. Consider hiring an annual complete cleaning and gel coat restoration. If your budget allows, you might want to look at having it done quarterly and then maintaining it yourself between the professionals.

Cleaning and maintaining teak wood on a boat

The exterior of our boat has a lot of teak wood, which means a lot of maintenance. We had no idea what we were doing when we started renewing the teak. And apparently, despite research and other people's advice, we didn't do the restoration properly. Our teak looks excellent now that we have the proper instructions and learned from our mistakes.

A couple of initial takeaways are this: don't expect the wood to look new. If you have an older boat, know that if the wood has not been adequately maintained, you will not likely return it to its original glory. Also, don't take any shortcuts. Do each and every step. Whether you follow these suggestions and do it yourself or get it done, the following protocol will leave you with a beautiful teak lasting many years.

Teak wood is one of the most popular materials used on boats. This is due to its durability and water-resistant properties, and the teak has an attractive appearance. But it is vital to maintain teak wood to look its best and ensure it lasts. Keeping it clean and conditioned will help with that longevity. When we got our boat, the wood had been in disrepair for many years. The owner previous to us had spent a lot of time and money to ensure the systems were in excellent order, but woodworking just wasn't his thing. So, we had a big project to undertake.

Remember that if your teak is in great repair, you might only have simple maintenance to perform. Alternately, you may have a lot of sanding and cleaning like us; we had deep grooves in the wood due to weather conditions beating up the wood. Honestly, it looked terrible.

Basic maintenance for oiled teak: Here are some steps to help you get started.

Clean the teak wood regularly: For teak that has been well maintained and has a good finish on it, simply remove dirt, grime, and other debris from the surface of the teak wood by using a soft-bristled brush and a mild soap solution. Do not use harsh cleaners or chemicals that could damage the wood or remove the conditioning oil. Always rinse the teak wood thoroughly with water after cleaning.

Keep the teak oiled: To protect the teak wood from weathering and maintain its natural golden color, apply teak oil using a soft cloth or brush. Be sure to follow the manufacturer's instructions for application and drying time. Typically, teak oil should be applied once every 3-4 months.

Once a year:

Sanding the teak wood: Teak can become weathered and grooved, losing its smooth texture over time. Use fine-grit sandpaper to restore the surface. Following the grain of the wood, lightly sand the surface, being careful not to sand too aggressively, as this could damage the wood. A light sanding once a year should be good, and not all surfaces must be sanded. Use your discretion and don't sand just to sand; otherwise, too much sanding will leave you railings that look like toothpicks over time.

Teak cleaner: Sometimes, it's best to use chemical cleaners if the teak wood has become heavily weathered and discolored. The teak cleaner will restore its beautiful appearance by removing the deep-set dirt and grime from environmental pollution, old teak oil, salt water, and cleaning residue. Follow the manufacturer's instructions carefully, as teak cleaner is an intense product. Be sure to rinse the teak completely after using the cleaner; do not allow any residue to remain. Also, wear gloves and eye protection. This stuff is no joke.

After a two-part cleaning process, you will want to give the teak another quick and super light sand using a 220 super-fine-grit.

Now, at this point, you may want to apply the teak oil according to the manufacturer's directions, or you might want to give the teak a longer-term finish. That is what we finally decided to do. When you apply any kind of shellac or varnish, follow the manufacturer's cleaning and preparation instructions, which should closely resemble the directions above. Apply a clear or light-colored sealant for the most natural teak look. Then, once thoroughly dried, apply 2-3 coats of a clear gloss coat. Be patient and wait for complete drying between coats. Also, don't wait too long between coats either. That's been our downfall. If done correctly, this process will allow for once-a-year maintenance of lightly sanding the top coat and then applying more coats. Some people apply 6-8 coats of varnish, but the product line we chose suggests only 2-3 coats. You can find product suggestions on our website.

Depending on where the teak is on your boat, cover the teak wood when not in use. Some people use rail covers during adverse weather conditions or when not using the boat. Since the teak on our boat is on doors, trim, rails, and steps, we keep ours exposed, thus necessitating regular cleaning.

These steps will hopefully keep your teak wood looking beautiful and ensure it lasts many years on your boat.

Keeping fit: Boat Workouts

———

Yoga for the Win

When you live aboard a boat, it can be hard to get proper exercise, especially when underway. While the space is limited, you can get a good workout on board; you must get creative.

The following are some exercises that are effective but don't require a lot of equipment or space:

Bodyweight-bearing exercises: Bodyweight-bearing exercises such as push-ups, squats, lunges, planks, and burpees are highly effective and can be done with limited space. However, you will want a bit more space to do any burpees. Try doing these on the aft (back) deck or in the saloon (living room), as both spaces will allow you to complete the exercises.

Resistance band exercises: Resistance bands are lightweight and take up hardly any space. They are perfect for working your upper body, lower body, and core. It is easy to find many exercises with resistance bands on YouTube or social media platforms.

Walking: Walking is one of the easiest ways to exercise and move if you live on a dock or have easy access to land. It gives you a chance to get outside and move around, and the best part is it doesn't cost a thing and doesn't require any equipment, just a good pair of supportive shoes.

Yoga is an excellent way to improve flexibility, balance, and core strength. It can be done on a mat or towel on the deck or in the saloon. In the next section, we have detailed poses that are easy to achieve in a limited space.

Swimming: If the weather and water conditions permit, swimming is an excellent exercise. It is the perfect exercise that provides a full-body workout and can help improve and maintain cardiovascular health. We are lucky enough to have a pool at our marina. Check into local health clubs or the YMCA if your marina does not offer a pool. Alternatively, if you are cruising somewhere with safe waters, by all means, dive in.

HIIT (High-Intensity Interval Training): **HIIT** workouts involve short bursts of intense exercise followed by small rest periods. They can be done using bodyweight exercises, resistance bands, or jumping rope. You can attempt this on board if you have the space on your boat. However, many marinas have a bit of grass or a parking lot where you can exercise. Try it early in the morning when the marina will be quiet often, and if you are in a warm climate, the temps haven't heated up yet.

We have found that Yoga is a great way to stretch, strengthen, and relax your body, even while on a boat. Our saloon (living room) is the perfect place to do some poses with minimal furniture rearranging.

Here are some yoga poses that can be done on a boat:

Mountain Pose: Stand with your feet hip-width apart, your arms at your sides, and your palms facing forward. Press your feet firmly into the floor and engage your core while lengthening your spine. Hold for 6-10 breaths.

Tree Pose: Stand on one foot, with the other foot placed on the opposite thigh. Press your foot into your thigh while you press your thigh into your foot. Bring your hands to your heart center and focus on a steady point before you. Hold for 6-10 breaths and repeat on the other side.

Downward-Facing Dog: Go down on the floor to all fours with your wrists lined up under your shoulders and your knees under your hips. Lift your hips up and towards the back while straightening your legs and arms. Press your palms into the floor and lengthen your spine. Hold for 6-10 breaths. Repeat as you feel necessary.

Cat-Cow Stretch: Come onto all fours again, with your wrists under your shoulders and your knees lined up under your hips. As you inhale, arch your back while raising your head and lower back (tailbone) towards the ceiling (Cow Pose). Then, as you exhale, round your spine while bringing your chin toward your chest (Cat Pose). Repeat 6-10 times.

Seated Forward Bend: Sit with your legs extended in front of you. Next, reach your arms up and lengthen your spine. Exhale while folding from your hips and reaching for your feet or shins. Keep your spine long and hold for 6-10 breaths.

Be sure to move slowly and mindfully on the boat. Be aware of your special restraints. If you have any medical conditions or are new to yoga or any other suggestions, consult a qualified yoga teacher or healthcare provider before practicing. Check out videos on the internet for a more detailed and thorough explanation of the different exercises mentioned.

How to Stay Connected

In this brief chapter, we review the internet and communication options.

Staying connected while living aboard can be challenging, but it's essential for staying in touch with loved ones, working remotely, or accessing critical services. As much as we would love to be disconnected, our schooling, work, and loved ones necessitate our need to be plugged in.

Here are some suggestions for staying connected:

Mobile Hotspots: Mobile hotspots allow you to connect to the internet using a cellular network. You can use a smartphone or tablet as a hotspot or purchase a dedicated hotspot device. Mobile hotspots are convenient, but their availability depends on the strength of the cellular network in the area.

Satellite Internet: Satellite internet is a reliable option for staying connected, using a satellite rather than a cellular network. This option is more expensive than mobile hotspots, and the connection quality may vary depending on the weather conditions and positioning.

Wi-Fi Extenders: Wi-Fi extenders can improve the Wi-Fi signal on your boat, allowing you to connect to Wi-Fi hotspots in the area. You can purchase a Wi-Fi extender designed for marine use or use a general-purpose extender. We have to use an extender on our boat as the marina wi-fi access can sometimes be spotty.

Marine VHF Radios: Marine VHF radios allow you to communicate with other boats in the area and access important weather information or emergency services. Some VHF radios also have GPS and AIS capabilities, which can help you navigate and avoid other boats in adverse weather conditions.

Cell Phone Boosters: Cell phone boosters improve the cellular signal on your boat, allowing you to make calls and access the internet more reliably. They work by amplifying the cellular signal and broadcasting it throughout the boat.

Satellite Phones: Satellite phones provide a reliable means of communication while living on a boat, using satellite connections rather than cellular networks. They are more expensive than cellular phones and require a subscription plan, but they provide reliable communication in remote areas.

Cooking on a Boat

This will be a much longer section, and probably one of the most frequently asked questions is how we cook on a boat.

When cooking on a boat, planning ahead, and making the most of the ingredients you already have are important. The limited storage space also means you can only stock up on ingredients that there's room for, so it's essential to be mindful and intentional with what you select.

Making frequent trips to the shops is not usually convenient, nor is it feasible. Living on a dock, we can run to the store, but there aren't often grocery stores or markets to stop off and pick up a few things if we are traveling. Learning how to provision a boat and what we need to have on hand at all times has been a learning experience.

We love to cook and try out new recipes, but our tiny galley (kitchen) does limit the space in which we can cook. The joke is that our galley is a one-butt kitchen—literally, only one person in the galley at a time. Fortunately, the galley has a full-sized refrigerator, freezer, massive cooktop, and oven. Even the built-in microwave is larger than the one we had in our last house. Those full-sized appliances meant that cupboard and counter space had to be sacrificed. Despite the lack of space, we like to cook food big on flavor and presentation.

Space may be in short supply, but we still make delicious food.

Here are some general tips for cooking with limited ingredients on a boat:

Stock up on staples: Keep a supply of staples like canned beans, tomatoes, pasta, rice, and grains like quinoa or couscous. These ingredients can be used as a base for many meals and stored easily in a small space.

Use canned or dried foods: Canned or dried foods have a longer shelf life and can be used to make various dishes. Canned tuna, salmon, or chicken can be used in salads, pasta dishes, or sandwiches. Dried fruits and mixed nuts can be added to breakfast oatmeal or in a bowl as a snack.

Get creative with spices: With limited ingredients, spices can flavor your dishes. Stock up on various spices, including salt, pepper, garlic salt, onion powder, and chili powder, and for the more adventurous, including curry, turmeric, paprika, cumin, and coriander. These can be used to season meats, vegetables, and grains. We love going to Trader Joe's and stocking up on interesting spice mixes, and the best part is spice bottles don't take up a lot of space.

Buy local produce: Local produce is often fresher and more affordable than imported produce, making it a great option for cooking on a boat. Look for farmers' markets or local grocery stores that carry local growers to stock up on fresh fruits and vegetables. The key is to use it right away. If we don't process or use fresh produce immediately, it can go to waste quickly. Meal prepping helps preserve freshness and less waste. Fresh isn't easy to get when underway, so rely on frozen produce. If you are really on the ball, freeze your produce in preparation for being off-dock.

Repurpose leftovers: This may seem a no-brainer but use leftover ingredients to create new dishes. For example, leftover cooked rice can be turned into a fried rice dish by adding vegetables, eggs, and soy sauce. Our family typically likes leftovers for lunch the next day, so it's not that often that our leftovers go to waste. Sometimes, we repurpose the leftovers, and making a great meal and less waste is almost always super satisfying.

Catch your own seafood: If you're out on the water, take advantage of the available fresh seafood or freshwater fish. Simple grilled fish dishes can be made with just a few ingredients and are delicious and healthy. Make some rice and steamed carrots, and have a healthy, fresh meal from the sea, river, or lake.

Ideas for easy one-pot meals for cooking in a small space.

As we've already pointed out, cooking in a small galley kitchen on a boat can be challenging, especially when dealing with limited counter space or a small stove. One-pot meals are a great solution to this problem since they allow you to prepare a complete meal using only one pot or pan.

Here are some easy and delicious one-pot meals that you can prepare in a small galley kitchen:

One-pot spaghetti: Cook spaghetti in boiling water until it's al dente (barely cooked). Drain the pasta and set it aside. In the same pot, sauté garlic and onions in olive oil until fragrant. Add canned tomatoes, salt, and pepper to taste and bring to a simmer. Add the cooked spaghetti into the pot and stir until the sauce is well combined. Serve with grated Parmesan cheese.

One-pot chili: Brown ground beef with chopped onions and garlic in a pot. Drain any excess fat. Add canned diced tomatoes, kidney beans, and chili powder. Simmer for 20-30 minutes until the flavors have melded together. Serve the chili with freshly grated cheddar cheese, then add a dollop of sour cream for taste and a sprinkle of fresh cilantro for garnish and added flavor.

One-pot chicken and rice: In a pot, sauté chicken thighs until browned on all sides. Remove from the pot and set aside. In the same pot, sauté chopped onions and garlic until fragrant. Add rice, chicken broth, and your favorite vegetables (like carrots and peas). Return the chicken thighs to the pot and bring to a simmer. Then cover and let cook until the rice is tender, and the chicken is thoroughly cooked. Season with salt and pepper to taste.

Another One-pot pasta e fagioli (beans): Sauté diced bacon until crispy in a pot. Remove from the pot and set aside. In the same pot, sauté chopped onions and garlic until fragrant. Add canned diced tomatoes, chicken broth, and a can of drained and rinsed cannellini beans. Bring the mixture to a simmer and add your favorite small pasta shapes, like penne or shells. Let cook until the pasta is tender. Serve with the crispy bacon on top.

One-pot beef stroganoff: Cook egg noodles first, then set aside in a covered bowl. In a pot, brown stew beef with chopped onions and garlic. Add a carton of beef broth and bring to a simmer. Add sliced mushrooms and a dollop of sour cream. Let cook until the beef is tender, and the sauce has thickened. Add salt and pepper to taste. Serve over the egg noodles.

More delicious recipes can be found on our website. Link at the end of the book.

Keeping Food Fresh

Creative ideas for storing food on a Boat: Another question we are frequently asked is how we keep food on a boat. Storing food on a boat can be challenging, especially because we have limited space. There is a lot of space to store things like pasta, rice, and other dry ingredients. We also can store canned goods, water jugs, and other items with a long shelf life, but again, the space has to be well utilized. We keep our toilet paper in a bin in the bilge and other household items, like backup dish soap, under one of the banquet seats in a storage space.

Being creative with the space is a challenge we are up for.

Use vacuum-sealed bags: Vacuum-sealed bags are an excellent option for storing food on a boat because they take up less space than traditional containers. They also help to keep food fresh for more extended periods. The drawback is having to store the machine and bags. Good storage food bags with a zipper closure are also a good option for storing food in the freezer if a vacuum-sealed bag system isn't for you.

Food dehydrator: Some boaters swear by having a food dehydrator. It allows you to dry fruits, vegetables, and meats, which helps to extend their shelf life. Dried foods take up less space and can be rehydrated when ready to use them. Again, the drawback to a food dehydrator is its storage space, and you also have to like working with dehydrated food. It's a great option if you like dehydrated fruit like my kids love dried fruit.

Stackable containers: Invest in good quality stackable containers, a great way to maximize your storage space on a boat. Look for containers that are made of durable materials and have tight-fitting lids. Look for containers that do not contain BPA (a harmful chemical that leeches into the food); if you see eco-friendly or bamboo containers, snatch them up. We have some containers made of bamboo and love them!

Store produce in net bags: Net bags are a great way to keep produce on a boat because they allow air to circulate around the food, which helps to prevent the produce from going bad. Hang the bags from hooks or other fixtures to keep them off the counter.

Other airtight containers: Airtight containers are essential for keeping food fresh on a boat. Look for containers with silicone seals that create an airtight barrier. Though I don't advocate using glass for storage, some people like using glass jars with hinged lids with a seal. This container is terrific for storing beans, rice, and loose pasta. It keeps the moisture out and the freshness in. Just be careful with the glass.

Consider investing in a refrigerator/freezer combo: A refrigerator/ freezer combo can be great. These appliances are designed to take up vertical space and help you keep food fresh for longer. We are fortunate to have a full-sized refrigerator/freezer in our galley, and I don't know what we would do without the freezer space. It is worth losing a bit of elbow room to accommodate a large refrigerator/freezer. For those who don't have the space to spare, invest in a good freezer that can be packed with frozen food.

Bins: We use bins with lids to stack. These bins are great for storing our dried goods and organizing our storage. On the outside of the container, we put a label with a list of what's inside to save on digging through everything to find an ingredient.

Long-term food storage can be easy if you take the measures to be organized and keep track of what you have. We finally took an inventory and kept it in a spreadsheet to stop buying duplicates. This has also allowed us to track where the gaps are in our supply. Also, dispose of manufacturer packaging whenever possible. The outer packaging is frequently either plastic or cardboard, which takes up extra space and contains manufacturing chemicals. Decant things like rice and beans and consolidate. Despite the lack of storage, by using space-saving containers and clever storage methods, you can utilize the space you have without skimping on your provisions.

Tips for organizing a small galley kitchen on a boat

Organizing a small galley kitchen on a boat can be challenging. Still, maximizing the available space and your kitchen area is possible with creative planning and smart storage solutions. Here are some tips to help you get started:

Keep it simple: Limit the number of pots, pans, and utensils you bring on board. Stick to versatile, multi-purpose tools that can be used for various tasks.

Use vertical space: Hang pots and pans from hooks or a pot rack mounted on the wall or ceiling. Use magnetic strips to keep knives and other metal utensils within easy reach.

Use corners: Corner shelves or rotating trays can store spices, condiments, and other small items.

Keep counters clear: Use wall-mounted or hanging storage to keep frequently used items, like cooking oils and spices, off the counter. Invest in collapsible or stackable storage containers to save space when not in use.

Use under-sink space: Install a sliding drawer or organizer under the sink to store cleaning supplies and other items that are not used frequently.

Optimize cabinet space: Use drawer dividers to keep utensils and flatware organized. Install shelves or stackable containers inside cabinets to make use of vertical space.

Store bulky items elsewhere: Store bulky appliances, like blenders or food processors, in a separate storage area to free up counter space.

Invest in multi-purpose items: Look for items that can be used for multiple purposes, like a cutting board that doubles as a sink or stove cover and a pot lid that can be used as a splatter guard.

Baking in a small galley kitchen

Yes, you can bake on a boat. Well, that's if you have an oven. If the galley does not have an oven, you can get a countertop convection oven or a toaster oven that allows you to use a bake setting. We keep a few extra appliances in the banquette seat storage to reduce clutter when not in use. Also, we have found that manufacturers have gotten smart and are now making baking pans that fit in small cookers like air fryers and toaster ovens. Look on Amazon or Walmart for some options.

Here are some tips to help you get started baking in your little galley:

Plan ahead: Ensure you have all the necessary ingredients and equipment before baking. Read the recipe carefully and make a list of what you need. Measure out your ingredients in advance to save on space.

Keep it simple: It's best to stick to simple recipes with fewer ingredients when baking in a small space. Quick bread, scones, muffins, cookies, and simple cakes are all great options.

Optimize your workspace: Counter space is at a premium in a small galley kitchen. Make the most of your workspace using a cutting board or silicone mat as a work surface. Use nesting bowls and measuring cups to save space.

Use a portable oven: As mentioned above, a portable oven is an excellent option for baking on a boat. These compact ovens can be used on a countertop and are available in various sizes. They're also easy to clean and can be stored in other areas of the boat when not in use.

Or use a convection oven: A convection oven can be a great option for baking on a boat. These ovens circulate hot air, which helps to cook food more evenly and quickly. They're also energy-efficient and can be used at lower temperatures than conventional ovens.

Our oven is large, uses a ton of energy, and puts out a lot of heat. We often use our countertop oven instead of the big oven.

Baking on a boat can take longer than in a regular kitchen. The boat may be rocking, and the oven may take longer to heat up. Be patient and allow extra time for your baked goods to cook. Also, it's not likely that you will be able to bake large batches either. For some, it might be a good thing to not have the option to indulge in a three-layer cake; I know that's a good thing in our case.

Essential Gadgets and Utensils for Cooking on a Boat

Working in a small kitchen doesn't mean we don't need the same tools for preparing food, the same as in a kitchen on land. It means we must be careful about what we bring onto the boat. Our limited space restricts the volume of tools and utensils, but it's incredible how we have discovered that we don't need the same volume of options when living in a house with a large kitchen. We love to cook, but fewer tools have not hindered creating yummy dishes in our tiny galley. If anything, we've become more creative.

Having the right tools and gadgets in your galley kitchen can make cooking on a boat much easier and more enjoyable. Here are some essential items for your boat kitchen tool kit:

Chef's knife: A sharp chef's knife is essential for chopping and preparing food on a boat. Look for a knife with a sturdy blade and comfortable grip.

Paring knife: An absolute must when preparing vegetables and fruit. The small serrated blade lets you cut through tomatoes' tough skin and slice and dice perfectly.

Wood Cutting Board: A durable cutting board protects your countertops and ensures safe food preparation. Look for durable bamboo, which does not absorb smells and food as much as other woods. Consider a cutting board that can be easily stowed away when not in use. Alternatively, we keep our cutting board next to the cooktop, which protects the countertop and provides a good work surface. Use a silicon BPA-free board for preparing meat. Our small one can easily be tucked away in a cupboard under pots.

Nonstick cookware: Nonstick cookware is great for cooking on a boat because it requires less oil and is easier to clean. Look for pots and pans with durable nonstick coatings. Watch the labels for ones that are not coated with chemicals. It should say something like PFOA-free, a harmful chemical used in many nonstick cookware.

Silicone utensils: Silicone utensils are heat-resistant and won't scratch your cookware. Look for a set that includes a spatula, spoon, and tongs.

Collapsible measuring cups and spoons: Collapsible measuring cups and spoons are great for saving space in a small galley kitchen. Look for sets that can be easily nested and stored.

Immersion blender: An immersion blender is a must-have! It's a versatile tool that can be used for making soups, sauces, and smoothies. Look for a lightweight model with multiple speed settings.

Mini Blender: We have a small drink blender perfect for making smoothies or shakes. It's similar to a Ninja but not as fancy and has a smaller price tag. It is ideal for stowing away in a cupboard, taking up about as much space as a large jar of peanut butter.

Mini food processor: We use ours constantly to chop herbs, dressings, pesto, cookie dough, and just about anything that needs to be chopped or combined. We got one that is small but has several attachments, allowing us to use it to make smoothie bowls.

Flat cheese grater: A handheld flat grater doesn't take up much space in the utensil drawer and is a must if you like to grate your own cheese instead of buying store-bought grated cheeses. Ours is flat and stores easily.

Wood spoons: We primarily use wood spoons for cooking. They won't scratch most surfaces, can be used for various purposes, from sautéing to stirring, and are easy to maintain. Again, look for bamboo utensils if possible, but other wood utensils are fine, just not as a renewable resource or eco-friendly.

Garlic press: Yes, we could chop the garlic really fine, but the garlic press makes quick work of mincing it, and it doesn't take up much space.

Stainless steel mixing bowls: Metal bowls are great for having on a boat and don't rust! Many manufacturers make them in multiple sizes that can be easily nested for storage. We prefer these to glass bowls for the breakage or chipping factor.

Corkscrew/bottle opener: A corkscrew/bottle opener is essential for opening wine and beer on a boat. Look for a model that is compact and easy to use.

With these essential tools and gadgets in your galley kitchen, you'll be well-equipped to prepare delicious meals on your boat. Don't forget to prioritize storage space and look for items that can be easily stowed away when not in use. Happy cooking!

Clothing Storage

We must admit that living aboard a yacht does not lend itself to having an expansive wardrobe. In fact, we all have a small wardrobe compared to the fully stocked walk-in closet we had on land. We have always been clothes enthusiasts and love having many options. Everyone in this family likes clothes; even the youngest likes having a lot of clothes. Living in a warm climate, we do not require cold-weather garments. Although we have to wear pants and jackets for about six weeks of the year.

So, instead of parkas and snow boots, we have beach hoodies, flippers, and wetsuits. So, you may wonder just how we overhaul our clothing and maximize our storage.

It goes without saying that Clothing storage on a liveaboard boat can be a bit challenging due to the limited space. We left behind all of our cold-weather clothing and gear in our storage unit. Should we need to go somewhere below fifty degrees, we still have the gear, albeit it's not easily accessible. Plus, the growing boys would require complete re-outfitting.

We are pleasantly surprised at the amount of space our boat provides.

To utilize that space more effectively, we use storage bags. The kind that is vacuum sealed to compress your clothing and make more space. These bags protect our clothes from moisture, mold, and mildew. We also used these bags for bedding and towels when moving across the country.

We also maximize our closet space. If your boat has closets or lockers, use them efficiently. You can install additional shelves or hanging bars to create more space. Consider using a hanging shoe organizer or sweater organizer to store small items. We also use pant hangers, which allow pants to cascade down, and several pairs can fit.

Folding clothes to efficiently save space is equally important. Use the method of folding clothes neatly and standing vertically rather than stacking them. This method saves on wrinkles and maximizes space. Another folding technique that minimizes each item's space is not folding but rolling. Take the garment and roll it like when packing a suitcase.

The most obvious way to maximize space is limiting the amount of clothing you own, but where's the fun in that? Despite our preference for options, we limit the clothing we bring on board. In fact, we often encourage the concept that when we bring something on board, something must leave by donating to the local charity store. We also focus on owning versatile items that can be worn in different ways, like a top that can be worn with shorts, pants, or a skirt. Investing in quality and more durable items also means it will last longer. The type of material that clothing is made of is equally important. Clothing made of breathable materials like cotton and linen will help prevent moisture buildup and reduce the chance of mold and mildew. Thus making it easier to store.

Use a storage ottoman in the salon or the main cabin if there's space. Storage ottomans can serve dual purposes: a place to sit and store clothing. We have one, but we have blankets and extra bedding instead of storing clothing. We've also seen some stray Legos in there, too.

Luckily, we have a washing machine and dryer on board because smaller wardrobes also mean doing laundry more frequently. We can dry most of our clothes outside on the deck when we are underway and not living on a dock. Drying clothes on the deck is usually frowned upon, so if you have to air dry, do so without it being an eyesore from the docks.

We do our best to keep our clothes to a minimum, which does not come naturally, but spending less time focusing on the things we own and enjoying our time aboard the yacht is worth the effort.

Checklist for Provisioning a Boat to Live Aboard

This is an essential list to get you started. Customizing this list to suit your needs will be necessary, especially once you have bought the boat and are preparing to move aboard. It can be overwhelming, so we've broken it down into categories.

Food and Beverages:

Non-perishable food items (canned goods, pasta, rice, cereals)

Fresh produce (fruits, vegetables)

Meat, poultry, and seafood (consider freezing options)

Dairy products (milk, cheese, yogurt)

Bread and bakery items

Snacks and desserts

Condiments, spices, and seasonings

Beverages (water, juices, sodas, coffee, tea)

Alcoholic beverages (if desired)

Basic Cooking and Kitchen Supplies:

Pots, pans, and cooking utensils

Cutting boards and knives

Mixing bowls and measuring cups

Baking sheets and oven-safe dishes

Can opener and bottle opener

Cooking oil, butter, and other cooking essentials

Food storage containers and zipper-closure bags

Plates, bowls, and utensils

Glasses, mugs, and cups

Dish soap and cleaning supplies

Water and Drinks:

Freshwater supply (consider capacity and storage)

Water filters or purifiers (if needed)

Water bottles and jugs for storage

Ice cubes or ice trays

Hot water kettle or coffee maker

Tea and coffee supplies (if desired)

Personal Care and Toiletries:

Toilet paper and tissues

Hand soap and hand sanitizer

Shampoo, conditioner, and body wash

Toothbrushes and toothpaste

Haircare products

Razors and shaving cream

Feminine hygiene products

Medications and first aid supplies

Sunscreen and insect repellent

Laundry detergent and fabric softener

Cleaning and Maintenance Supplies:

All-purpose cleaner

Disinfectant wipes

Paper towels and cleaning cloths

Broom, mop, and dustpan

Vacuum cleaner or handheld vacuum

Trash bags and recycling bags

Spare light bulbs and batteries

Essential tools for minor repairs

Lubricants and cleaning solvents

Safety Equipment and Supplies:

Life jackets and personal flotation devices

Fire extinguishers

First aid kit

Emergency flares and signaling devices

Flashlights and headlamps

Smoke and carbon monoxide detectors

An emergency backup power source (portable generator or battery)

Miscellaneous:

Bedding and linens (sheets, blankets, pillows)

Towels and washcloths

Clothing and personal items

Entertainment items (books, games, DVDs)

Navigation charts and guidebooks

Boat documentation and paperwork

Spare parts for the boat (fuses, belts, filters)

Spare fuel containers (if needed for things like outboard motors)

Dock lines and fenders

It's important to consider the duration of your provisioning needs and the storage space available on your boat. Consider dietary restrictions, preferences, or specific requirements when preparing your provisioning checklist. Regularly review and restock your provisions to stay on top of replacing items consumed.

Challenges of Living Aboard a Yacht

This idyllic existence also comes with its fair share of challenges. In this chapter, we'll explore some of the significant challenges living on a boat presents, including navigating storms and adverse weather, dealing with health emergencies, and coping with the isolation that can sometimes come with life on the water.

Navigating Storms and Adverse Weather: One of the most formidable challenges of yacht living is confronting the unpredictability of Mother Nature. Storms and adverse weather conditions are inevitable and can be particularly daunting at sea.

Weather Forecasting: Staying informed about weather forecasts is paramount. Modern technology provides access to real-time updates, enabling boaters to plan their routes and take precautions when necessary.

Seamanship Skills: Boaters must develop excellent seamanship skills, including knowing how to handle a yacht in rough seas and maintaining safety during storms.

Safety Equipment: Well-equipped yachts carry essential safety gear such as life vests, EPIRBs (Emergency Position Indicating Radio Beacons), and storm sails to prepare for unexpected weather events.

Resilience and Adaptability: Mentally preparing for the challenges of storms is equally important. Adapting to changing conditions and remaining calm is essential for safety and peace of mind. Also, be prepared and have plans, including contingencies, to ensure your safety and well-being.

We've lived through two hurricanes now, one worse than the other in terms of potential severity and the effect they were to have on the area. We literally moved all of the items of value and things we didn't want to deal with replacing and took this stuff to the grandparent's house. We were fortunate to have that as an option. Many boaters who live aboard don't have the option of staying with family when disaster strikes. We are blessed and fortunate to have options in place. Further, we were incredibly blessed to have been spared the devastation experienced in neighboring communities. A disaster plan should be made, and contingencies should be prepared.

Health Emergencies at Sea

Just as on land, health emergencies can occur at sea, but they often come with unique challenges due to isolation and limited access to medical facilities.

First Aid Training: Every boat should have a well-appointed first-aid kit, and at least two people should be trained in basic first-aid techniques. First responders may be hours or even days away, so stabilizing injuries and illnesses is crucial. You want two people to know basic skills in case one of the two is the one injured. Take it several steps further and train the entire crew; if you have a family, everyone should know some basics to help ensure survival in an emergency.

Communication: Boat radios, satellite phones, and other communication devices can be lifesavers during health emergencies. Learning how to use them correctly is important. Again, this is something multiple people aboard should know how to use. As mentioned earlier, make a list of contacts in case of an emergency. These numbers are a valuable asset.

Medical Evacuation Plans: You should have well-planned evacuation plans in case of severe medical emergencies. This includes knowing the nearest ports with medical facilities and the procedures for summoning help. If you are miles away from land, minutes count, and being aware of your options and how to receive help may be lifesaving.

Health Maintenance: Preventing health issues is the best approach. Prioritize health and wellness by getting plenty of sleep, eating nutritiously, staying hydrated, and exercising regularly.

Coping with Isolation and Solitude: Isolation is good and bad in yacht living. While the solitude can be serene, it can also be isolating, especially during long voyages.

A few ideas on how to cope with long voyages and mental stability are below:

Crew (Family) Dynamics: Practice open communication. Encourage teamwork and mutual support, all of which can help mitigate feelings of isolation. The expedition will be more manageable if the family or other crew members are in sync, especially when on long hauls.

Stay Connected: In our digital age, staying connected to loved ones and the world is easier than ever. Satellite internet and communication tools can keep you connected. Use those tools to your advantage and stay in touch with those important to you.

Hobbies and Entertainment: Busy yourself with hobbies that can be conducted on a boat, such as sewing, knitting, painting, and reading. Pursuing interests can provide mental stimulation and avoid isolation-related boredom.

Mental Resilience: Keep your brain active. You can create mental resilience with something as simple as meditation and mindfulness.

Those practices can be beneficial to keeping centered and having the strength to work through long days on a passage.

Cruising on a yacht would seem to be enough of an exciting adventure to keep your mental health in check. However, for some, the limitations that come with this type of lifestyle can be debilitating. The journey should be fulfilling and exciting by preparing for the challenges ahead and using the tools and skills you put in place.

Environmental Considerations When Boating

Boating is not just a recreational activity; it's a unique connection to the world's waterways. It's an experience that should be appreciated, not taken for granted, and preserved for future generations.

As we head out on our adventures or if we stay on the dock, we must do so responsibly, with a commitment to environmental conservation.

Here, we will dive into the critical aspects of environmental responsibility in boating. With a focus on sustainable boating practices, we will also look at reducing our environmental impact and wildlife conservation.

Sustainable Yachting Practices

Sustainable yachting practices are the foundation of responsible boating. Here are some key points to consider:

Eco-Friendly Power Generation: Many yachts are equipped with solar panels, enabling them to harness renewable energy sources. By relying on clean energy, you reduce your carbon footprint and minimize the impact on marine ecosystems. If you do not currently have solar panels, consider having them installed. It will also save you money on power while on the dock and allow you to be off-grid whenever you choose. The up-front cost might be a little daunting initially, but it will pay for itself in no time. Also, don't let the professionals talk you into more than you need. Get enough to power the items that you want but select a system that can be scaled should you choose to boost your power down the road.

Efficient Fuel Management: Fuel consumption is a significant contributor to environmental issues. Fuel-efficient boating can be achieved by optimizing engine performance, keeping the systems clean and running efficiently, and avoiding unnecessary idling.

Waste Management: Proper disposal of waste is paramount. Install and use wastewater treatment systems to minimize the discharge of pollutants into the water. Always adhere to local regulations regarding waste disposal, and never discharge sewage or hazardous materials into the waterways. Keep your disposal systems in optimal cleanliness and working order.

Responsible Anchoring: In sensitive marine environments, such as coral reefs or seagrass beds, anchoring can cause significant damage. Use designated anchorages and mooring buoys whenever possible and employ appropriate anchoring techniques to avoid damaging the seabed.

Reduce Plastic Usage: Single-use plastics severely threaten marine life and the planet. Ditch the plastic bottles, go reusable whenever possible, and check into water filtration systems that can be installed. We use a system that allows our water to be highly filtered, thus boosting our confidence in refilling our metal water bottles. For long-term water storage on board, get containers rated for potable water storage. These containers may often be made of plastic, but look for the ones that allow for long-term use and are void of the chemicals shown to leech into the water. You can search the internet for sources for purchasing these types of long-term storage containers in various sizes.

Fishing with Integrity: Adheres to catch limits and size regulations if you enjoy fishing. Try catch-and-release if you aren't fishing for food. Also, avoid overfished areas to protect the balance of marine ecosystems. You can go to your state's fish and wildlife website for detailed information about what is allowed and how to adhere to their guidelines. Also, ensure you have paid for your fishing license for a day or the whole year; you must pay for usage. It may seem trivial, but your license fee helps to pay for keeping our waterways clean and safe for all to enjoy.

Reducing your environmental impact goes beyond sustainable practices; it involves a mindful approach to boating:

Slow Down: Reducing speed can significantly decrease fuel consumption and emissions. Slower travel allows you to enjoy the journey, take in the scenery, and decrease the risk of collisions with marine life and other boaters.

Use Navigational Apps: Modern navigation technology provides real-time weather data, tidal information, and route optimization. Utilize these tools to plan safer and more efficient voyages.

Practice Sustainable Provisioning: Choose locally sourced, sustainable, and organic foods when provisioning your boat. Minimize food waste by planning meals and properly storing food.

Water Conservation: Freshwater is a precious resource at sea. Install water-saving fixtures on your boat, fix leaks promptly, and be mindful of water usage when showering or doing dishes. Consider using towels multiple times and hanging them to dry on the deck. Some boats even have water catchment systems. If you plan to be off-dock for some time, that might be something to consider, especially if you don't have a water maker aboard.

Wildlife Conservation

Yachts often travel over marine environments filled with diverse wildlife. Here's how you can contribute to wildlife conservation:

Maintain Safe Distances: When encountering marine mammals, birds, or other wildlife, maintain a safe distance to avoid disturbing them. Observe without intruding and never attempt to catch or touch.

Don't feed the Wildlife: Feeding wildlife can disrupt their natural behaviors, lead to dependency on human food, and harm their health. Do not feed any animals you encounter.

Environmental responsibility in boating is not just a choice; it's a moral obligation. By practicing sustainable boating methods, reducing your environmental impact, and actively participating in wildlife conservation efforts, you can ensure that the beauty and wonder of our world's waterways remain intact. As boaters, we are not just passengers on these seas; we are privileged to use these waterways and need to do our part.

Travel Planning

Below are some suggestions for different trips to various regions of the United States. These are all trips that we would love to embark on. Depending on your location, one of these trips might interest you. Each trip includes details on where to start, dockage suggestions, points of interest with websites, addresses, and coordinates. Call ahead to make reservations for dockage if it's high season to ensure you will have a slip ready that will be able to accommodate your needs. If you are a mooring ball or anchoring fan, the same is true if you want to utilize a marina's facilities. The dockage mentioned in each passage is only a suggestion. Later in this guide, you will find a list of resources for finding dockage worldwide and in your neck of the woods.

When heading out, don't forget to leave a float plan.

A float plan is a written communication that provides essential information about a boat voyage, typically given to a responsible person or authority before departing.

The plan should include details such as the departure point, destination, expected arrival time, the boat's description, the number of people on board, emergency contacts, and other pertinent information. The purpose of a float plan is to enhance safety and aid in search and rescue efforts in case of an emergency, ensuring that someone knows your whereabouts and can initiate assistance if needed.

Include a picture of the vessel with the float plan. Providing a digital and a printed copy of both the plan and the picture is good practice.

You can leave the float plan with the office at the marina, where you are home-based, with family or friends.

Also, consider a paid membership to Sea Tow, which provides emergency services on the water. Think AAA, but on waterways. Check out **seatow.com** for more information about what services they provide.

New York to Nantucket Island Cruise:

Starting Point: New York City, New York

Dockage: Nantucket Boat Basin, Nantucket, MA

Points of Interest: Explore Nantucket's historic downtown, visit the Whaling Museum (nha.org/visit/whaling-museum), and relax on the island's pristine beaches.

Coordinates: Start at 40.7128° N, 74.0060° W.

Charleston to Savannah Coastal Journey:

Starting Point: Charleston, South Carolina

Dockage: Savannah Yacht Club, Savannah, GA

Points of Interest: Enjoy the charm of Savannah's historic district, explore Bonaventure Cemetery (visitsavannah.com/things-to-do/Bonaventure-cemetery), and savor Lowcountry cuisine.

Coordinates: Start at 32.7765° N, 79.9311° W.

Chesapeake Bay History Tour:

Starting Point: Annapolis, Maryland

Dockage: Inner Harbor Marina, Baltimore, MD

Points of Interest: Visit the U.S. Naval Academy in Annapolis, explore Baltimore's Inner Harbor (baltimore.org/neighborhoods/inner-harbor), and tour historic Fort McHenry (nps.gov/fomc).

Coordinates: Start at 38.9784° N, 76.4887° W.

San Diego to Catalina Island Escape:

Starting Point: San Diego, California

Dockage: Two Harbors, Catalina Island, CA

Points of Interest: Dive at the Avalon Underwater Park (visitcatalinaisland.com/activities-adventures/scuba), explore Catalina's rugged interior and relax on its beautiful beaches.

Coordinates: Start at 32.7157° N, 117.1611° W.

Florida Keys

Starting Point: Miami, Florida

Dockage: Key West Historic Seaport, Key West, FL

Points of Interest: Snorkel at Dry Tortugas National Park (nps.gov/drto), visit the Hemingway Home (hemingwayhome.com) and enjoy the lively atmosphere of Duval Street.

Coordinates: Start at 25.7617° N, 80.1918° W.

Chicago to Milwaukee Great Lakes Adventure:

Starting Point: Chicago, Illinois

Dockage: McKinley Marina, Milwaukee, WI

Points of Interest: Explore Milwaukee's lakefront, visit the Milwaukee Art Museum (mam.org), and enjoy local craft breweries.

Coordinates: Start at 41.8781° N, 87.6298° W.

Outer Banks:

Starting Point: Beaufort, North Carolina

Dockage: Manteo Waterfront Marina, Manteo, NC

Points of Interest: Visit the historic Roanoke Island (roanokeisland.com), explore the Cape Hatteras National Seashore (nps.gov/caha), and watch wild horses on Shackleford Banks.

Coordinates: Start at 34.7179° N, 76.6638° W.

Seattle to Vancouver Island Expedition:

Starting Point: Seattle, Washington

Dockage: Victoria Inner Harbor Marina, Victoria, BC, Canada

Points of Interest: Explore Butchart Gardens (butchartgardens.com), visit the Royal BC Museum (royalbcmuseum.bc.ca), and experience the charm of Victoria.

For this trip, be prepared for customs clearance when entering Canada.

Coordinates: Start at 47.6062° N, 122.3321° W.

Gulf Coast from Mobile to New Orleans:

Starting Point: Mobile, Alabama

Dockage: New Orleans Municipal Yacht Harbor, New Orleans, LA

Points of Interest: Enjoy the cuisine of the French Quarter, explore the Garden District, and

experience the vibrant music scene.

Coordinates: Start at 30.6954° N, 88.0399° W.

San Francisco Bay to Monterey

Starting Point: San Francisco, California

Dockage: Monterey Harbor, Monterey, CA

Points of Interest: Visit the Monterey Bay Aquarium (montereybayaquarium.org), explore

Cannery Row and go whale watching in Monterey Bay.

Coordinates: Start at 37.7749° N, 122.4194° W.

Rhode Island to Martha's Vineyard

Starting Point: Newport, Rhode Island

Dockage: Vineyard Haven Harbor, Martha's Vineyard, MA

Points of Interest: Visit the Gingerbread Cottages in Oak Bluffs, explore Edgartown, and enjoy

fresh seafood.

Navigation Tip: Be aware of strong tidal currents around Martha's Vineyard.

Coordinates: Start at 41.4901° N, 71.3128° W.

Tampa Bay to the Florida Keys

Starting Point: Tampa, Florida

Dockage: Marathon Marina & RV Resort, Marathon, FL

Points of Interest: Snorkel at Sombrero Reef, visit the Dolphin Research Center (dolphins.org),

and relax on Marathon's beaches.

Navigation Tip: Look for manatees in the Intracoastal Waterway.

Coordinates: Start at 27.9506° N, 82.4572° W.

New Jersey Shoreline Escape:

Starting Point: Atlantic City, New Jersey

Dockage: Cape May Harbor, Cape May, NJ

Points of Interest: Visit Cape May's historic district, explore the Cape May County Park & Zoo

(capemaycountynj.gov/1034/Zoo), and relax on Cape May Beach.

Coordinates: Start at 39.3643° N, 74.4229° W.

Before these trips, checking current conditions, weather forecasts, and local regulations is essential. Consult nautical charts to ensure your boat is in good condition. Hiring a local guide or captain for added safety and navigation support might be a good idea for some.

Safe travels!

Finding a Slip-A Resource Page

10 Websites to find available slips domestically and worldwide for transient and permanent liveaboard.

1. Dockwa: This platform allows boaters to search, reserve, and pay for transient slips and moorings at marinas in various locations. www.dockwa.com

2. Snag-A-Slip: provides a comprehensive database of marinas and offers an easy-to-use online booking system for slip rentals in the United States, Canada, the Caribbean, and beyond. www.snagaslip.com

3. Marinas.com: offers an extensive database of marinas worldwide, including slip availability, amenities, and reviews from boaters. It also provides a reservation system for some marinas. www.marinas.com

4. Marina Reservation: Another database of marinas worldwide. www.marinareservation.com

5. PierShare: A platform that connects dock owners and boaters to one another and is fully automated for booking management. www.piershare.com

6. RentMySlip: A source for finding or listing boat slips for rent or sale. www.rentmyslip.com

7. Boatsetter: While primarily known as a boat rental platform, Boatsetter also offers slip rentals in specific locations. It connects boat owners with available slips through its online platform. www.boatsetter.com

8. Airbnb for Boats: Airbnb for Boats is an online platform allowing boat owners to rent out their boats and offer slip accommodations in various locations. Website: www.airbnb.com/(search for "Boats" in the accommodation type) This is also a great opportunity to test yacht living without the long-term commitment.

9. Marinalife: Provides an extensive directory of marinas in the United States, Canada, Bahamas, and the Caribbean. While it focuses on providing marina information and services, it may not offer direct slip bookings. It is a good resource for finding marina information and a means to contact for bookings. www.marinalife.com

10. Navily: A community-based platform allowing boaters to discover and book berths in marinas across Europe and other international locations. It also provides reviews and information about marinas. www.navily.com

Boat Terms, Definitions, and Glossary

It helps to know the difference between port and starboard and what an aft deck is. Below is a basic list of yacht and boating terms. This list covers many of a yacht's common exterior features and components. Since yachts vary widely in size and design, additional terminology may be specific to particular types of yachts and sailing vessels.

Exterior Yacht Terminology:

Anchor: A heavy device used to secure the yacht to the seabed.

Bow: The front of the boat.

Bow Pulpit: The railing or structure at the bow.

Bow Thruster: A propulsion device in the bow used for maneuvering.

Bilge: The lowest part inside the hull where water collects.

Boot Stripe: A painted stripe along the waterline to enhance the yacht's appearance.

Bulwark: The protective barrier on the sides of the deck, often with a railing or handrail.

Cleats: Fixtures on the deck used for securing lines.

Cockpit: An open area at the rear of the yacht used for steering and crew activities.

Davit: A crane-like structure used to hoist and lower tenders or other equipment into the water.

Deck: The top surface of the yacht.

Deck Hardware: Various fittings, including cleats, winches, and hatches, for securing lines and

accessing the interior.

Gunwale: The top edge of the bulwark or hull sides, where the deck and sides meet.

Hatch: An opening in the deck providing access to the interior.

Helm: The steering station.

Hull: The main body of the boat.

Hull Paint: The outer layer of paint is applied to the hull for protection and aesthetics.

Hull Port: A window or opening in the hull for ventilation or aesthetic purposes.

Hull Sides: The vertical sections of the hull between the bow and the stern.

Hull Windows: Transparent openings in the hull for natural light and visibility underwater.

Keel: The bottom part of the hull that provides stability.

Nameplate: A decorative or informational plaque with the yacht's name.

Pilothouse: The area where the yacht's navigation equipment and controls are located. It may

include seating for guests.

Port: The left side of the yacht when facing forward.

Porthole: A circular window on the side of the hull.

Pushpit: A similar railing or barrier at the stern of the yacht.

Rudder: The movable fin or board at the stern that controls the yacht's direction.

Stern: The rear of the yacht.

Stern Rail: The railing or structure at the stern.

Stern Thruster: A similar device at the stern for improved maneuverability.

Swim Platform: An extended platform at the stern for swimming and boarding.

Toe Rail: A safety rail along the edge of the deck to prevent crew and passengers from falling

overboard.

Transom: The flat, vertical surface at the stern.

Transom Door: A hinged door at the stern for boarding.

Wet Bar: A small bar area typically found in the salon or on the deck for serving drinks.

Wheelhouse: The area where the yacht's navigation equipment and controls are located. It may

include seating for guests.

Winch: A mechanical device for winding in lines or sheets.

Windlass: A machine used for raising and lowering the anchor.

Sailboat specific terms:

Backstay: The wire or cable supporting the mast from the stern.

Boom: The horizontal pole attached to the mast controls the mainsail's angle.

Clew: The corner of a sail to which a sheet is attached.

Cleat: A device used to secure lines.

Forestay: The wire or cable supporting the mast from the bow.

Genoa: A large foresail that overlaps the mast.

Halyard: A line used to hoist sails.

Jib: A headsail positioned forward of the mast.

Main Sail: The primary sail, typically attached to the mast.

Mast: The vertical pole that holds the sails.

Masthead: The top of the mast.

Sails: Collective term for all the canvas on a yacht.

Sheet: A line used to control the angle and trim of sails.

Shroud: Wire or cable support running diagonally from the mast to the hull.

Interior Yacht Terminology:

Aft Berth: A cabin at the stern with a berth.

Berth: A sleeping area or bed.

Bulkhead: The interior wall of the yacht.

Cabin: Individual rooms or sleeping quarters within the yacht for passengers and crew.

Cabinetry: Storage compartments and cabinets.

Chart table/Navigation Station: An area with navigation charts, instruments, and communication

equipment for the crew to monitor the yacht's course and safety.

Companionway: The steps or ladder leading to below the deck.

Companionway Hatch: This hatch covers the entrance to the cabin below.

Dinette: A table with seating for dining, often in the galley area.

Freezer: A colder storage unit than the refrigerator.

Galley: The yacht's kitchen is equipped with appliances, countertops, and storage for food

preparation and cooking.

Galley Stove: The cooking appliance in the galley.

Head: The yacht's bathroom or toilet facilities, including a sink, toilet, and sometimes a shower.

Headliner: The ceiling inside the yacht.

Hanging Locker: A closet for hanging clothes.

Locker: A storage compartment or closet.

Nav Station: The navigation station or area inside the yacht.

Pullman Berth: A folding or retractable bed that can be stowed away to create more space when

not in use.

Refrigerator: A cold storage unit for food.

Salon: The main living area of the yacht, often located amidships, features seating, entertainment

systems, and sometimes a dining area.

Settee: A long, cushioned bench or seat.

Sink: A basin for washing dishes and hands.

Stateroom: A high-quality, often luxurious cabin for guests or owners, typically featuring a bed,

seating, and private facilities.

V-berth: A forward cabin with a V-shaped bed.

Vanity: A small table with a mirror and storage for personal care.

Motor yachts are equipped with various systems and electronics to ensure safe and comfortable

operation, navigation, and onboard amenities. Here's a detailed list of some critical systems and

electronics commonly found on a motor yacht, which you will want to familiarize yourself with.

Some of the items listed below may be duplicated from the list above. Just work with it, as

sometimes repetition is sometimes a good thing.

Navigation and Communication Systems:

AIS (Automatic Identification System): Allows for identifying and tracking nearby vessels.

Chart plotter: A display unit that shows electronic charts and the yacht's position.

Electronic Compass: Provides precise heading information.

GPS (Global Positioning System): Provides accurate position information for navigation.

Radar: Uses radio waves to detect objects and other vessels, especially in low visibility conditions.

Satellite Communication: Offers global communication capabilities for voice, data, and internet

access.

SSB Radio (Single Sideband Radio): Provides long-range communication capabilities for offshore

and international voyages.

VHF Radio: Used for communication with other vessels and emergency services.

Weather Monitoring: Weather radar, barometers, and anemometers monitor weather conditions.

Engine and Mechanical Systems:

Bow and Stern Thrusters: Aid in docking and low-speed maneuvering.

Bilge Pump System: Removes excess water from the hull to prevent flooding.

Engine Monitoring and Control System: Displays engine parameters like temperature, RPM, and

fuel consumption.

Exhaust System: Manages engine exhaust emissions and noise.

Fuel System: Includes fuel tanks, filters, and transfer systems.

Generator: Provides electrical power for onboard systems and amenities when the main engines

are not running.

Main Engines: The primary propulsion system is usually powered by diesel or gas engines.

Water Maker: Converts seawater into fresh drinking water.

Electrical Systems:

Batteries: Store electrical power for use when the engines and generators are off.

Battery Charger: Recharges the yacht's batteries when connected to shore power or the generator.

Electrical Panel: The central control point for all onboard electrical systems.

Inverter: Converts DC (battery) power into AC power for appliances and outlets.

Shore Power Connection: When docked, The yacht can connect to onshore power.

Safety and Security Systems:

Fire Suppression System: Automatic or manual systems to extinguish onboard fires.

Smoke and Carbon Monoxide Detectors: Ensure early detection of hazards.

Security Cameras: Monitor the exterior and interior of the yacht.

Burglar Alarm: Alerts crew to unauthorized access.

Life Rafts and Life Jackets: Safety equipment for emergencies.

Entertainment and Comfort Systems:

Audio/Video System: Includes TVs, speakers, and media players for entertainment.

HVAC (Heating, Ventilation, and Air Conditioning): Climate control for interior comfort.

Galley Appliances: Refrigerators, stoves, ovens, microwaves, and dishwashers.

Satellite TV: Provides access to television programming.

Wi-Fi and Internet: Enables onboard internet access.

Interior Systems:

Central Vacuum System: Makes cleaning easier.

Freshwater System: Provides fresh water for drinking and bathing.

Interior Control Systems: Control panels for lighting, HVAC, and other amenities.

Interior Lighting: Various lighting fixtures for ambiance and functionality.

Plumbing System: Includes freshwater and wastewater systems, toilets, and showers.

Waste Treatment System: Manages and treats wastewater.

Window Blinds and Shades: For privacy and light control.

Deck and Exterior Systems:

Anchor Windlass: Controls the anchor deployment and retrieval.

Davits and Crane Systems: For launching and retrieving tenders and water toys.

Deck Washdown System: Provides pressurized water for cleaning the deck.

Exterior Lighting: Navigation lights, deck lights, and underwater lights.

Hydraulic Passerelle: Extends from the yacht for boarding and disembarking.

Hydraulic Stabilizers: Reduce yacht roll and improve onboard comfort.

Sunroof or Convertible Top: For open-air or covered deck areas.

Swim Platform and Ladder: For easy access to the water.

Tender and Toy Storage: Space for storing smaller boats and water toys.

Yacht Types and Features:

Aft Cabin: A cabin located at the rear of the yacht, typically reserved for owners.

Catamaran: A yacht with two parallel hulls, offering stability and space.

Flybridge: An open area on the top deck of a motor yacht, often with a helm station.

Gelcoat: The outer layer of fiberglass on the yacht's hull.

Ketch: A two-masted sailing yacht with a taller main mast and a shorter mizzen mast.

Saloon: The main interior living space of the yacht.

Sloop: A single-masted sailing yacht with one headsail.

Trawler: A motor yacht designed for long-distance cruising and fuel efficiency.

Trimaran: A yacht with three hulls, providing stability and speed.

Here's a detailed list of glossary terms often encountered when buying a yacht:

Acceptance Period: A specified time during which the buyer can inspect and accept the yacht.

Broker: A yacht broker is a professional who assists in buying or selling yachts.

Closing: The final stage of the purchase when ownership is transferred.

Deposit: An initial payment to secure the yacht during the purchase process.

Listing Agreement: A contract between the owner and the broker to list the yacht for sale.

Purchase Agreement: A legally binding document outlining the terms of the yacht purchase.

Sea Trial: A test run of the yacht to evaluate its performance and handling.

Surveyor: A marine expert who assesses the yacht's condition before purchase.

Financing and Insurance:

Down Payment: The initial amount paid by the buyer before financing.

Hull Insurance: Coverage for damage or loss to the yacht itself.

Liability Insurance: Coverage for damage or injury caused by the boat.

Loan-to-Value Ratio (LTV): The percentage of the yacht's value that can be financed.

Marine Lender: A financial institution that provides loans for yacht purchases.

Title Insurance: Protection against legal claims to the yacht's ownership.

Registration and Documentation:

Certificate of Documentation (COD): A federal registration for U.S. vessels.

Certificate of Origin (COO): Proof of the yacht's origin and manufacturer.

Flag State: The country where the yacht is registered, often chosen for tax and regulatory reasons.

Hull Identification Number (HIN): A unique serial number for the yacht.

Other Ownership Structures:

Bareboat Charter: A leasing arrangement where the lessee is responsible for all aspects of the

yacht.

Fractional Ownership: Co-ownership of a yacht by multiple parties.

Yacht Management Company: A service that handles maintenance and crewing for yacht owners.

Crew and Crewing:

Captain: The person responsible for operating and navigating the yacht.

Crew: The individuals responsible for maintaining and servicing the yacht.

Steward/Stewardess: Crew members responsible for guest service and housekeeping.

Maintaining and servicing a yacht involves various tasks and glossary terms related to multiple

aspects of care, from cleaning and waxing to more specialized functions like bottom cleaning

and teak maintenance.

Here's a detailed list of glossary terms associated with yacht maintenance and servicing:

Maintenance and Repairs:

Boatyard: A facility where yachts are hauled out and serviced.

Dry Dock: A facility where the boat can be lifted out of the water for maintenance.

Haul Out: Lifting a yacht out of the water for inspection and maintenance.

Maintenance Schedule: A planned timetable for regular maintenance tasks.

Marine Surveyor: A professional who assesses a yacht's condition for buyers, insurance, or

maintenance purposes.

Preventive Maintenance: Routine tasks are done to prevent issues before they occur.

Winterization: Preparing the yacht for storage during the off-season.

Exterior Maintenance Terms:

Anodes/Zincs: Sacrificial metal pieces that protect against galvanic corrosion.

Antifouling Paint: A special paint applied to the hull to deter marine growth.

Bottom Cleaning: Hiring a diving crew specializing in scraping the bottom of boats to remove

growth like algae, barnacles, and clams.

Bottom Paint: Paint applied below the waterline to prevent fouling.

Compounding: Abrasive polishing to remove oxidation and scratches from the gel coat.

Hull Cleaning: Removing algae, barnacles, and marine growth from the hull.

Hull Inspection: Examining the hull for damage, blisters, or cracks.

Polishing: Buffing the yacht's surfaces to enhance shine.

Teak Maintenance: Care and cleaning of teak wood surfaces.

Waxing: Apply wax to the hull for protection and a glossy finish.

Interior Maintenance Terms:

Bilge Cleaning: Cleaning and maintaining the bilge to prevent odors and contamination.

Deep Cleaning: Thorough cleaning of all interior spaces.

Galley Maintenance: Cleaning and servicing the kitchen area.

Head Maintenance: Servicing toilets and sanitation systems.

HVAC Maintenance: Servicing heating, ventilation, and air conditioning systems.

Interior Upholstery Cleaning: Cleaning and treating fabric and upholstery.

Water System Flushing: Flushing freshwater tanks and lines.

Engine and Mechanical Terms:

Battery Maintenance: Care of yacht batteries, including charging and testing.

Cooling System Service: Servicing the engine's cooling system.

Engine Service: Routine maintenance, including oil changes and filter replacement.

Exhaust System Maintenance: Inspection and cleaning of exhaust components.

Fuel System Service: Cleaning and maintaining the fuel system.

Transmission Service: Maintenance of the transmission system.

Electrical Systems Terms:

Electrical Inspection: Checking all wiring, connections, and components.

Electronics Calibration: Calibrating navigation and communication equipment.

Generator Service: Maintenance of onboard generators.

LED Conversion: Upgrading lighting to energy-efficient LED fixtures.

Safety Equipment Terms:

Fire Suppression System Inspection: Servicing fire suppression systems.

Flare Replacement: Replacing expired flares.

Life Raft Inspection: Checking the condition of onboard life rafts.

Rigging and Sail Maintenance Terms:

Rigging Inspection: Checking the condition of standing and running rigging.

Running Rigging Replacement: Running rigging will be replaced as needed.

Sail Repair: Repairing torn or damaged sails.

Safety Equipment Inventory: Ensuring all safety gear is on board and in good condition.

Winch Service: Maintenance of sailboat winches.

Tender and Water Toy Terms:

Jet Ski Service: Maintenance of onboard jet skis

Paddleboard/Kayak Maintenance: Care for onboard paddleboards and kayaks.

Tender Maintenance: Servicing and maintaining the yacht's tender.

Final Recommendations for Preparing to Live Aboard a Boat

Before heading out on this great adventure, complete the checklist covering essential aspects such as skills, certifications, legal requirements, and documentation. Some things on this list are required, whereas others are merely recommendations.

Skills and Knowledge

Basic Seamanship Skills: Learn essential skills like navigation, boat handling, anchoring,

docking, and understanding the maritime rules of the road.

Resources: Local sailing schools, boating courses, or online tutorials.

Safety Training: Acquire basic first aid, CPR, and water safety knowledge to handle emergencies

on board.

Resources: Red Cross courses, local community centers, or boating safety courses.

Weather Forecast Interpretation: Learn to interpret weather forecasts and understand weather

patterns affecting boating conditions.

Resources: Online weather courses, meteorology books, or marine weather apps.

Mechanical and Engine Maintenance: Familiarize yourself with basic engine maintenance,

troubleshooting, and minor repairs.

Resources: Engine manuals, boating courses, or workshops offered by marinas.

Certifications

Boating Certifications

Obtain certifications like the U.S. Coast Guard Auxiliary's Boating Skills and Seamanship

Certificate or equivalent relevant to your region.

Resources: U.S. Coast Guard Auxiliary, Royal Yachting Association (RYA), or local boating

authorities.

Sailing Certifications

Consider obtaining certifications like the RYA Competent Crew or the American Sailing

Association (ASA) certifications for sailing knowledge and skills.

Resources: RYA, ASA, or reputable sailing schools.

Legal and Documentation Requirements

Vessel Registration: Ensure your boat is properly registered with the appropriate maritime

authority in your country.

Resources: Local maritime authorities or government websites.

Boating Licenses: Check if your region requires a boating license or permit to operate a boat

and obtain it if necessary.

Resources: Local boating authorities or government websites.

Insurance: Acquire comprehensive yacht insurance to cover accidents, damages, and liability.

Resources: Insurance brokers, maritime insurance companies, or online insurance providers. Some carriers may require you to have a boater's resume, simply a statement of your past boating experience. Include in this resume the boats you have had, size, year, make, and how many hours of boating you have from each boat. Also, include any courses or other relevant experience. An example of a boater's resume is included in the back of this book.

Mooring and Docking Permits: Determine whether you need permits for mooring or docking

in specific locations and obtain them accordingly.

Resources: Local marinas, harbor masters, or relevant governmental agencies.

Documentation

Vessel Documentation: Keep your boat's registration documents, insurance policy, and any other legal documentation in a secure and easily accessible location on the boat. We recommend keeping copies in a dry storage bag at the navigation station or helm inside the boat.

Personal Identification: Have copies of your identification, passports, visas (if applicable), and other personal documentation stored in a waterproof and secure location. Make sure it is handy if you need to access those documents quickly.

Emergency Contacts: Compile a list of emergency contacts, including marine towing services, local authorities, and important phone numbers for quick access during emergencies.

Resources and Recommendations for Liveaboard Yacht Living

You'll find that a wealth of resources and a network of fellow liveaboards can be invaluable. This list provides a guide to online resources, forums, yacht living associations, and additional gear and equipment recommendations to enhance your liveaboard experience. All links and websites were accurate at the time of publication. If they are no longer available, use the keywords for an internet search.

Online Resources

Cruising and Sailing Forums

Cruisers Forum (www.cruisersforum.com): An active online community where sailors and

liveaboards discuss everything from boat maintenance to cruising destinations.

SailNet (www.sailnet.com): Offers information, articles, and an active forum for sailors of all

levels.

Weather and Navigation

NOAA's National Weather Service (www.weather.gov): Provides up-to-date weather forecasts,

marine weather warnings, and charts for U.S. waters.

Navionics (www.navionics.com): Offers navigation charts, apps, and tools for planning routes

and tracking your journey.

Boat Maintenance and Repairs

BoatUS (www.boatus.com): A valuable resource for boat maintenance tips, DIY repairs, and

information on marine insurance.

Practical Sailor (www.practical-sailor.com): A trusted source for unbiased boat reviews, gear

recommendations, and maintenance advice.

Yacht Living Associations

Seven Seas Cruising Association (SSCA) Website: (www.ssca.org) SSCA offers valuable

resources, forums, and a sense of community for cruisers and liveaboards.

American Sailing Association (ASA) www.asa.com) ASA provides sailing education,

certifications, and a network of sailing enthusiasts, including liveaboards.

Cruising Club of America (CCA) Website: [cruisingclub.org](www.cruisingclub.org) CCA

promotes the sport of offshore cruising and offers educational programs and resources for

members.

Additional Gear and Equipment Recommendations

Safety Equipment: We've mentioned many times that safety equipment is essential. Check out

these places for places to acquire.

EPIRB (Emergency Position-Indicating Radio Beacon (www.acrartex.com): A vital tool for

sending emergency distress signals.

Life Raft (www.switlik.com): Invest in a quality life raft with proper servicing intervals.

Communication Gear

VHF Marine Radio (www.icomamerica.com): Ensure reliable communication with other vessels

and emergency services.

Satellite Phone (www.iridium.com): Stay connected, even in remote areas.

Navigation Tools

Handheld GPS (www.buy.garmin.com): A portable GPS device is a valuable backup for navigation.

Binoculars with Stabilization (www.fujifilm.com): Stabilized binoculars are essential for spotting

hazards and distant landmarks.

Entertainment and Comfort:

E-book Reader (www.amazon.com/kindle): Save space and weight with an e-book reader for a

library of books on board.

Solar-Powered Ventilation Fans (www.westmarine.com): Keep your cabin well-ventilated and

comfortable.

Safety and Security:

Marine Fire Extinguishers (www.fireboy-xintex.com): Ensure you have the right type and number

of fire extinguishers on board.

Bilge Pump Alarm (www.rulepumps.com): Monitor the bilge for water accumulation with an

alarm system.

Environmental Considerations:

Portable Solar Panels (www.goalzero.com): Generate renewable energy to reduce environmental

footprint.

Eco-Friendly Cleaning Products (www.biokleen.com): Choose biodegradable and eco-friendly

cleaning supplies to minimize harm to aquatic ecosystems.

These resources and recommendations provide a solid foundation for your liveaboard yacht living experience. Explore the online communities, join associations, and equip your yacht with essential gear and equipment to ensure a safe, comfortable, and enjoyable journey on the water. As you immerse yourself in the liveaboard lifestyle, you'll discover additional resources and connections to enhance your adventure.

FIND US

Lastly, if you have made it this far, we sincerely thank you for your support. Buying this book helps us keep our liveaboard lifestyle afloat.

Consider joining our email list, which you can sign up for on our website at: http://www.cruisingschatzy.com

Follow us on Instagram @crusingschatzy[1].

Check out our videos on YouTube @crusingschatzy[2].

We would love to hear from you! If you need more information or have questions, please contact us through our website!

For downloadable documents mentioned throughout the book, go to our website: http://www.cruisingschatzy.com/helpfulresources for access to free downloads and more product recommendations.

Additional Resources Used

Google.com

Wikipedia.org

uscgboating.org

---

1. http://www.instagram.com/cruisingschatzy

2. https://www.youtube.com/@cruisingschatzy